JUST MY STORY

LEN HUTTON
has also written

CRICKET IS MY LIFE

The season opens—getting ready for the first practice

JUST MY STORY

LEN HUTTON

LONDON
HUTCHINSON

Hutchinson & Co. (Publishers) Ltd.
178-202 Great Portland Street, London, W.1
London   Melbourne   Sydney   Auckland
Bombay   Johannesburg   New York   Toronto

First published 1956

Made and printed in Great Britain by
TAYLOR GARNETT EVANS & CO., LTD.
BUSHEY MILL LANE
WATFORD, HERTS.

CONTENTS

LIST OF ILLUSTRATIONS

FOREWORD BY H. S. ALTHAM

BROADCAST made by Mr. H. S. Altham, Treasurer of M.C.C. and Chairman of Selection Committee during Len Hutton's captaincy of England, on 17th January, 1956, the day Hutton announced his retirement from first-class cricket:—

"I feel sure that every cricket-lover in the country was hoping against hope that by the time next season started Len Hutton would be and would feel himself fit enough to return to the game, and would once again open the innings for England against—I'm sure Australia won't misunderstand me if I call them our cricket enemies number one—but it is not to be and tonight we realize that a great chapter in the history of cricket is closed. Whether you look at the runs he made or the way he made them Len Hutton is secure of his place in cricket history. In Test Matches he scored more runs than any English batsman except Walter Hammond: he made the highest individual score in those games—his 364 at the Oval, in 1938: he has scored more runs in a single month than anyone in the game—1,294 in June 1949—and incidentally, he got another 1,000 runs in August. And until a week or so ago he held with Cyril Washbrook the record of 359 for an opening Test Match partnership. He made more hundreds than W.G. and to me at least that still means a good deal, and do not forget that but for the war he would probably have made thirty or forty more. His batting in the last three matches of the West Indies tour was completely decisive in drawing that rubber in one of the greatest rearguard actions in cricket history.

But tonight those who know him will be thinking less of such figures than of the man and the method that made them. I feel it is true to say that as a batsman he represented the complete development of modern technique, confronting the new problems posed by the bowler and the new field dispositions that support him.

He was, I think, basically a backfoot player, supremely

watchful and a master in killing the turning and lifting ball with the dead bat. Like all great batsmen, he never committed himself to a stroke until the last possible moment and like all great batsmen he gave the impression of playing a great deal with his hands.

But if defence was the basis of his batting, he was also a master of brilliant stroke play. I was lucky enough to see the whole of his famous innings of 364 at the Oval; and even now I do not know what I admired the more: the wonderful tenacity of his concentration and the resource of his defensive technique throughout all those thirteen hours of batting, or the balance and beauty of his cover driving and cutting which not even the great Australian fielding side could contain. He could, when the situation demanded, play every attacking stroke, and the Australians still talk of his sixty-two out of 122 on an impossible wicket in the Brisbane Test of 1950.

Yes—whether in technique or in the mental and moral resources that must reinforce it—Len Hutton was one of the very great batsmen of all time.

But of course he was something more than that. He was the first professional captain to lead an M.C.C. England eleven overseas, and perhaps tonight his proudest memory will be that under his captaincy England never lost a rubber. To captain England is a great challenge and never before so great as now in this age of remorseless publicity, when millions of people are following the fortunes of each match not only from the ring but from their own arm-chairs, whether with their eyes or their ears: and remember that when the M.C.C. asked Hutton to take their team to the West Indies he had had virtually no experience at all of captaining a side. He must, I am sure, have had many misgivings, for experience counts for so much in captaincy, and the problems to be faced are not confined to the field of play. But he brought to his job two vital assets—a very shrewd brain and a complete devotion to his task.

If in the West Indies his own batting, more than anything else, saved us, I believe that in Australia it was his tactical skill and determination that made ultimate victory possible after that fearful disaster at Brisbane which might well have undermined the morale of any side.

On that tour I know he was often fighting against physical disability and pain. But his courage carried him through, and his team and every cricketer in England will be always grateful to him.

And now he has taken his pads off, but with us the memories will remain of great innings played, of great matches which they have saved or won, but perhaps, most of all, of devoted service to the game which he has loved and adorned."

(Reproduced by permission of the B.B.C.)

TRADITION GOES OVER THE LORD'S BALCONY

"PRAY God, may no professional ever captain England!" I was nine years old when, in 1925, the late Lord Hawke, most celebrated of Yorkshire's amateur cricketers, uttered those momentous words. Nearly thirty years later, I became the first professional to be chosen by M.C.C. to lead England on the cricket field.

I realize that in his often misinterpreted sentence, Lord Hawke was merely saying that he hoped the day would never come when the supply of first-class amateurs capable of captaining England would run out. I appreciate as much as anyone the great contribution our famous amateurs have made to English cricket and the easier approach to captaincy that comes with not having to rely on the game for a living.

But inevitably those words made the England captaincy seem a very distant and unattainable thing to a humble Yorkshire professional and I may perhaps be allowed to say that I am a very proud man now. The captaincy of England has been the greatest honour bestowed on me during my twenty-one years as a first-class cricketer.

In this book I do not intend to go over the ground I covered in my autobiography *Cricket Is My Life*. There I told the story of my early years, of the encouragement I got from so many people, and of my development to become England's established opening batsman.

Here I want to deal with the newer story for, believe me, the captaincy of England, by amateurs or professional, is a whole book of interest, excitement, worry and wonder in itself.

I think the telling of the real story, the balancing of so many half-truths which have already hit the headlines, and the revealing of many stories about which only I knew, will be of interest to thousands who share my love of this great game of ours.

Let me make clear that I have never regretted joining that fine body of sportsmen who are the backbone of the game in this country. Cricket has been my life. But the captaincy of England was something I never dreamed of even after I had achieved almost every other honour in the game.

Somewhere around 1951, however, in company with a good many others, I began to sense that a change in the qualifications previously required for the captaincy of England was more than just a possibility.

Yet, I knew that in a country such as England, where tradition governs so many things, almost a revolution in our way of thinking would be needed to bring about such a change in the conservative cricket world. I suppose the two wars had something to do with the change which did come. Such upheavals were bound to carry with them some of the firmly rooted traditions to which English people had clung for so long.

After the 1939–45 war people began to argue that, if someone who had risen from the ranks was good enough to lead an army regiment in the field of battle, professional cricketers could be good enough to lead England in the field of sport. I heard these arguments without venturing an opinion.

Those who advocated a switch to a professional captain supported their case by pointing to England's post-war record. England failed to win a Test in the 1946–47 series in the first post-war tour of Australia—we lost three and drew two games —and we lost four and drew one of the five when the Australians came to England in 1948.

Two years later, in Australia, England lost four Tests and won one. Thus our overall record for fifteen Test matches with the Australians in three series was: won one, drawn three, lost eleven.

England had been led against Australia during this period by Wally Hammond, Norman Yardley and Freddie Brown, all top-class cricketers and personal friends of mine. They scarcely could be blamed if England were not good enough. A skipper can only do so much; the rest is up to the team.

Wally Hammond had given up his professional status before the war and had turned amateur before captaining England. I was determined never to take a similar step. When I was sounded on the subject on my return from Australia in

1951 my reply was: "If I am to captain England I will do so only as a professional."

Were the Selectors even then thinking seriously of throwing tradition over the Lord's balcony and appointing a professional captain? To me such a step seemed scarcely likely. Indeed, the approach made to me in London suggested their intentions were quite the contrary.

In any case I believed that, if the Selectors were toying with the idea of a professional captain, they would turn to Denis Compton, who had been vice-captain to Freddie Brown on the 1950–51 tour.

These were my thoughts in the spring of 1952 and though there had been much talk in the Press about my chance of being appointed, I could still scarcely believe my ears when Norman Yardley, chairman of the Selectors and captain of Yorkshire, rang me on a Sunday afternoon and asked: "Will you captain England in the First Test against India?"

Besides recognizing the importance as well as the honour of being the first professional to be cricket captain of England, I was well aware that if I did well I might lead my country in the Tests against Australia in England the following year.

No doubt the Selectors were looking that far ahead; they were trying to plan the conquest of Australia, in a cricketing sense, by way of India, and to do so they were taking the gamble of entrusting the leadership of the team to a man, not from one of the great Universities, but a village and club cricketer from the Yorkshire mill-town of Pudsey. I was honoured indeed.

I felt that an opportunity had been given to me to serve cricket and the professional cricketer as had been given to few men. It was a challenge I was prepared to meet to the limit of my ability. My immediate task was to captain England against India; the problem of winning back the Ashes from the Australians might come to me next. With the help that I knew would be given to me unstintingly by Selectors and players alike, and the support I was confident would come from the public, I desperately wanted to succeed.

*   *   *

What better Selection Committee could a newly appointed skipper wish to serve with than that composed of Norman

Yardley, Bob Wyatt, Freddie Brown and Leslie Ames, all of whom had much practical experience of Test cricket and a deep knowledge of the game?

They had been appointed in 1951 and re-appointed in 1952 and their ultimate goal from the start was to build up an England team for the 1953 series.

The Selection Committee were a solid combination of tip-top men, each so flexible in his approach to a problem that all were able to co-ordinate their views admirably.

Few men can claim a better technical knowledge than Bob Wyatt. Possessed of a defence that was well-nigh perfect, he was, in his prime, one of the most difficult batsmen in cricket to dismiss. Yet he never 'sat-on-the-splice' at Selectors' meetings; his judgment was always eminently sound.

The wealth of experience accumulated by Norman Yardley and Freddie Brown sometimes was cloaked by a lighthearted, happy-go-lucky attitude towards things which might have hidden their real qualities from casual acquaintances; but I knew and appreciated their value. Their views could be nothing but beneficial to a 'new boy' like me.

The help of Leslie Ames was equally valuable. A fellow professional who had been through the heat of Test battle forty-seven times in his playing days, he never betrayed excitability. Nothing rattled Leslie Ames. Any tendencies to the contrary soon pass on to the players.

The Selectors left no doubts that my task as captain was to win matches on the field and that their assistance would be confined to matters off the field. Accordingly, when the match had started they refrained from offering me advice on tactics and other matters connected with the game. These comments were made only at Selection Committee meetings which I, as captain, always attended. I welcomed all their suggestions and criticisms at such meetings and appreciated the trust they placed in my judgment on the field and in the dressing-room.

Let me say that for Selectors of the England side to be constantly visiting the dressing-room to offer advice to the captain or to any of the team could be most confusing to the players. Such advice would be given solely in the interests of the side but, to my mind, the Selectors help more by leaving matters in the hands of the man they appoint to lead the team.

Early photographs on and
off the field

Dorothy has been a great help

As an illustration of the unanimity of views among the Selectors on this point I cannot do better than recount the happening in the First Test at Nottingham when Freddie Brown was asked a tactical question by a reporter. He replied: "I don't know, I haven't been in the dressing-room since the match began. Go and ask Len."

Immediately after my appointment as captain, a preliminary meeting of the Selectors was called at which we discussed the names of about sixteen players likely to be required for the Tests. The capabilities of these men were already known to the Selectors, who did not need to maintain a close and constant watch on them. Selectors are much more concerned in studying the form and assessing the potential of the younger players, and they try to see as much as possible of them in order to obtain the maximum of information and background. Much of this can be obtained from discussions with county captains, although, I assure you, due allowance is always made for the captain's natural leaning either towards, or against, his own players.

Therein lies the advantage of appointing a Selection Committee composed of men from widely separated parts of the country. The Selectors are able to give first-hand information with the minimum of delay, and those who are active cricketers probably have played in matches against young players under consideration. No one could be better qualified to pass opinions than such selectors.

Some people are always drawing the attention of the Selectors to the qualities of certain players, very often quoting figures to improve the chances of inclusion of these individuals. What such enthusiasts often forget is that they, from their seats along the boundary, are not so well acquainted with the players as are the Selectors.

The Selectors know a man's record but they, too, know his temperament for the big occasion. Temperament for county cricket is vastly different from that required for Tests, a factor which in recent years has been well demonstrated. Besides that, figures, whether for bowling or batting, usually tell only half the story. Conditions of wicket, state of match, strength of opposition, size of grounds—all have to be taken into consideration. For instance, a Northamptonshire off-spinner who takes

B

five for 50 against Surrey on a good batting pitch at Northamp-
ton—a batsman's haven as a rule—probably has bowled just
as well, if not better, than a Yorkshire off-spinner who has
taken eight for 20 on a treacherous Bradford pitch against,
say, Essex.

*   *   *

Meetings of Selectors have been known to last as long as
seven or eight hours, which is no surprise to me now.

I always hoped to have players of the right temperament
in the England team. Trevor Bailey, Godfrey Evans, Alec
Bedser, Denis Compton, Brian Statham and Johnny Wardle
are the type I like to see in a Test side. All possess the ines-
timable virtue of being able to rise to an occasion and not fall
down because of its importance.

Having settled upon the Test team the Selectors always
pick a 'shadow-side', not necessarily an eleven that could take
the field *en bloc* but sufficient reserves to duplicate every position.
The big trouble in 1952 was, and still is, that when the
Selectors chose a 'shadow-team' they always found many more
players from whom to select than for the Test side itself. This
was caused by the falling-away from the high standard demanded for inclusion in the England eleven. Lowering the
standard slightly, as was essential, opened the door to many
more entrants. We could have picked a third team without a
tenth of the difficulty of choosing a first team.

A point that fireside Selectors often overlook is the importance in modern cricket of fielding. An international side
in present cricket cannot afford to 'carry' any passenger in
the field.

After all, good fielding can make all the difference between
winning and losing a Test or, indeed, a whole series, and many
a good batsman or bowler has had to be ruled out because of
his fielding limitations.

*   *   *

From the first, I knew I had the full confidence of the
Selectors and I willingly accepted the captaincy on a match-to-
match basis. I appreciated that, except when the great C. B.

Fry demanded the captaincy of the series in 1912, and got it, match-to-match selection has always been the custom.

My main concern on taking over the captaincy in 1952 was to search for two fast bowlers.

When I looked ahead to the Tests against Australia the following year I thought back to such great fast bowling combinations as Gregory and Macdonald, Lindwall and Miller, Larwood and Voce. They, more than any of their colleagues, had dominated Test scenes, and I was convinced that, on the easy-paced pitches so common in modern Test cricket, the biggest weapon for either side was a *pair* of top-speed bowlers of international standard. My hope was that England could produce such a pair.

I am convinced that a *pair* of quality fast bowlers make a far more potent weapon than one brilliant fast bowler supported by someone of much lesser pace. The absence of a second fast bowler affords a batsman some respite. Indeed, he can be shielded from the fast bowler's attack.

When two fast bowlers are bowling at the same time, the timid player is allowed no rest. No batsman of my knowledge 'likes' playing against really fast bowling but some are astute enough to show their dislike less than others.

My contention has always been that if a Test side has not two good fast bowlers their biggest chance of victory is in the possession of two slow bowlers capable of spinning the ball sharply, like Clarrie Grimmett and Bill O'Reilly, perfect examples of spin bowlers used by Australia to win Test matches before the war.

In 1952, England did not have two spinners comparable with Grimmett and O'Reilly. Some bowlers had regularly taken their hundred wickets a season in first-class cricket, but any who could be thought likely to command success on Test wickets was virtually non-existent. Since that time Jim Laker, Tony Lock and Johnny Wardle have benefited from experience and improved out of all knowledge, as their figures show.

The hunt for a pair of fast bowlers was not easy but the result was anything but discouraging. My main hope centred on Brian Statham, who went to Australia in 1950–51, and Freddie Trueman. I regarded Alec Bedser as a dual-purpose bowler, and a great one on rain-affected wickets. Yet, although

Alec was then indispensable to an English side, he was not a *fast* bowler and, with him in the team, only one fast bowler could be included in a balanced side. If two fast bowlers of real quality had arisen earlier the problems about Alec which arose in Australia in 1954–55 might have come to the fore earlier than they did.

In any fast bowler stamina and direction are essential qualities towards success. No one ever cultivates the latter without possessing the former. In 1952, however, Freddie Trueman lacked stamina. He was then only twenty-one and I estimated that he could not get to the top of his profession for another four or five years.

Much as I believed in his possibilities, his introduction to Test cricket in 1952 was made, therefore, sooner than I had hoped. If at the time England had not been short of great fast bowlers, Freddie might well have been left to mature in less strenuous pastures.

Yet, despite my feeling that Trueman was not sufficiently mature, he met with immediate success. Few will easily forget his eight wickets for 31 runs in the Manchester Test. My view was that this was too good to be true. The helpful pitches on which he bowled in Tests that season, coupled with the vulnerability of the Indian batsmen against fast bowling when the ball lifted abruptly or went through quickly, made Freddie look to be a better fast bowler than he was, at that stage of his career.

Freddie was, in a sense, my protégé. When he came into the Yorkshire county side at the age of eighteen, I realized his infinite potential and I devoted hours and hours talking to him, both on and off the field. Often I fielded at mid-off, where I was able to watch the batsmen more closely and advise Freddie how and where to bowl to them.

At that time, being very young, and with a physique far from developed, Trueman was inclined to tear up to the crease and just sling the ball down without due regard for length or direction. He had a fine action for a fast bowler and he could, occasionally, make the ball run away from the bat, but he was raw and undeveloped. Whatever his limitations, however, I admired his spirit. He had the determination so essential to a fast bowler and he had a fast bowler's 'temper'—

he looked upon batsmen as personal enemies. On the field that is a virtue. Cricketers who 'love' the opposition on the field rarely do well against them.

Unfortunately, too much was expected of Trueman in 1953 as a result of his successes against India in 1952. As he was by then on National Service, he was short of practice for first-class cricket and could not keep himself in tip-top form.

In his unit matches in the R.A.F. he was sure of a regular bag of five or six cheap wickets every innings by merely bowling as fast as he could but that was not ideal preparation for big cricket.

When I thought about him, however, I cast my mind back to 1946 when I had my first encounter with Ray Lindwall. Then Lindwall was not only a great fast bowler; he was a completely mature one as well.

Very often a young player loses his form after his introduction to Test cricket. Sometimes this happens for only a short period, occasionally the loss of form lasts longer. Then his struggle to get back will depend upon both his ability and his temperament.

The step from first-class cricket to Test cricket is more difficult than many imagine. The young player will find that he no longer can expect to face fairly easy bowling from one end or, if he is a bowler, he cannot be certain of bowling often to batsmen vulnerable against his special brand of bowling. In fact, Test cricket against the top countries is hard work from start to finish, and any results achieved by a Test player are done so only in combat with players every bit as good as, or better than, himself.

The young player whose early Test results do not live up to all the preliminary publicity and expectations surrounding him may lose some of his confidence—and with it his form. His struggles, which he alone can master—albeit with the help and encouragement of his friends—start when he sets out to regain the road to the top. This time if he arrives again at his destination he is likely to be a far more matured player and one able to treat the twin imposters of triumph and disaster with greater equanimity.

So it was with Brian Statham. He went to Australia midway through the 1950–51 tour largely on the recommendation of Cyril Washbrook and myself. After going out straight from an English mid-winter he found the heat of Australia too great a contrast to be able to overcome immediately and he did not meet with the success hoped. He took some time to rise to the heights which Cyril Washbrook, in particular, forecast for him from the start of Brian's career, but subsequent events proved Cyril was right. Brian is today the best fast bowler in the world.

The name of Cyril Washbrook inevitably throws my mind back to the crisis when I opened the England innings with him from 1946 to 1951. In that time we began England's innings in three Test series against Australia, 1946–47, 1948 and 1950–51, and I confess that I felt that taking the first brunt of the Lindwall-Miller explosions was to suffer an experience somewhat akin to being in the 'blitz'. These two magnificent fast bowlers seemed to be throwing everything at us except the rockets from Woomera. England's opening attack, by comparison, was a most unseasonable example of peace on earth and goodwill to all men.

Take 1948 as an illustration of the friendly nature of England's opening attack. Because of the complete absence of fast bowlers, England went into the Fifth Test at the Oval with Alan Watkins, no more than medium-paced, to open the attack with Alec Bedser. This happened after Ray Lindwall and Keith Miller had shot England out for fifty-two. Poor Alan did his best but, apart from his lack of pace, he was suffering from a badly bruised shoulder, the result of being hit by a Lindwall flyer when batting, and his speed was still further reduced. Even so, I doubt whether his medium-paced bowling would have troubled Australia on what was, despite England's score, a good batting wicket. As a result, the Australian batsmen had all the time in the world to deal with him.

The three series against Australia to which I have referred were the most exacting in my career as a batsman but they did one important thing to me—they convinced me that England must find a similar *pair* of fast bowlers capable of blasting our way to victory. How we came to find them, not immediately, but nearly three years later, I must leave for a while to recount the other stages in England's progress towards first the recovery then the retention of the Ashes. Before I leave the subject of Miller and Lindwall, however, I should reveal that fraternization between the rival combinations, Lindwall-Miller on the one hand, and Washbrook-Hutton on the other was strictly limited. For their part, I always noticed that when the appeals of Ray and Keith for decisions against Cyril and me were turned down by the umpires, they looked clearly annoyed even though they seldom made any comment. For our part, we said very little, either on or off the field. Keith Miller did not fail to notice this and once he remarked: "I cannot understand why Len Hutton dislikes me."

Today, eight years later, I can answer the question. Keith, you were too good a bowler for me to 'like' you.

During my Army service I often found difficulty in accustoming myself to an 'on-and-off parade' technique. Likewise, I could not be over-friendly off the field with two men, Lindwall and Miller, who had given me more sheer hell on it than I care to remember.

When either of them had the ball ready to bowl to me I felt that, temporarily at any rate, they just 'hated my guts'.

I must emphasize that I have the highest regard for them, and all other Australian cricketers, either on or off the field. I admire the Australians' approach to the game; they have the utmost ability for producing that little extra, or instilling into the opposition an inferiority complex that can have, and has had, a crushing effect. Australians have no inhibitions. They respect a fighter—but woe betide the weak-kneed!

When I took over the captaincy England had batting as well as bowling problems. Since the war, the batting had broken down repeatedly against quick, shock bowling. My task was to try to remedy this by helping to find men who could face up and play Lindwall and Miller with some hope of success. To my mind, one of the biggest blunders made was to discard Cyril Washbrook after the Australian tour of 1950–51. In particular, England could have done with his experience against Australia in 1953; he was, I thought, still one of the world's best opening batsmen.

However, I did not receive the necessary support when I pressed Cyril's claims at meetings of the Selection Committee, and I was not prepared, single-handed, to make an outright

demand for his inclusion, as Bob Wyatt had done in the case
of Tommy Mitchell of Derbyshire for the Second Test against
South Africa at Lords in 1935. Unfortunately for Bob Wyatt
his insistence was not rewarded by the events of the match.
South Africa won by 157 runs, their first victory in a Test
Match in England in a period of twenty-eight years. And
Tommy Mitchell's match analysis was three for 164!

Those who said that Cyril Washbrook could not be over-
keen on playing again for England following his 'No-Yes'
change of front before the 1950-51 tour to Australia were
able to sway those who were undecided. A great opening
batsman, one with whom I had been associated so many times
for England, was thus passed over, to my considerable regret.

In his place England needed someone with ability to 'take
off the shine' from the new ball and, simultaneously, pave the
way for the later batsmen. Unless someone capable of doing
this could be found the Selectors knew that little scope would
exist for the later batsmen whose duty was to press on with the
scoring.

Since Cyril Washbrook was passed over for Test cricket
the problem of England's opening pair has never been solved.
Of course, England inherited the problem from the first-class
counties. Positions one and two in the batting remain the most
difficult to fill in all grades of first-class cricket, yet I believe
that the task of opening an innings is no harder today than
before the war. The main trouble is that so many modern
batsmen decline both the honour and the responsibility of
going in first. Most of them prefer to bat when the ball has
lost its gloss.

If England could find two opening batsmen capable of
putting on even fifty runs once every two innings little more
would be expected of them.

In 1953 we needed a sound opening pair to handle Messrs.
Lindwall and Miller, unlimited. How successful we were can
be estimated from the remarkable fact that not since Cyril
Washbrook and I were together have England found a pair
of openers able to stay at the crease until lunch time!

CHAPTER II

END OF A TWENTY-ONE-YEAR-OLD 'HOODOO'

THE Australians came to England in 1953 fairly confident of their ability to retain the Ashes they had held since 1934. They had every cause to be. England had failed in successive attempts, here and in Australia, to beat them in any Test series in the previous twenty-one years.

The last time England beat Australia in a Test series was in 1932–33 when Douglas Jardine led the side in the tour which gave rise to the 'body-line' controversy. It was always in my mind that victory then was founded on the fast bowling of Larwood and Voce.

I was only sixteen when these two superb fast bowlers burst so dramatically upon the scene. Twenty-one years later I was captain of England, and hoping somewhere to discover a pair of fast bowlers as good as Larwood and Voce who could accomplish in England what Douglas Jardine's men did on the faster wickets of Australia.

On the 1953 tour of England the Australians were led by Lindsay Hassett, a thoroughly likable man in every way, a 'born cricketer' as that distinguished writer, Mr. Neville Cardus, once described him, and a personality in the game. I was keen to obtain as much first-hand information about the Australians as possible and to do this I travelled to London and met the Australians at their hotel. Lindsay Hassett was not anxious to talk there surrounded by so many people and he suggested we should adjourn to the 'little pub round the corner'.

Conversation there became light (unlike the beer the Australians had demanded), but it wasn't just beer in which Lindsay Hassett and his team-mates were interested. They were only too eager to talk 'shop' to find out as much as they could about the men they were likely to play against on the tour. They showed particular interest in the young men whom they had not encountered, such as Peter May, Freddie Trueman and Tony Lock.

I hope I left the Australians with no doubt about England's ability to recover the Ashes. After my experience in Australia in 1950–51 I felt that England's main task would be to keep a close check on Neil Harvey and find an effective counter to the shock bowling of Ray Lindwall and Keith Miller.

I knew only too well that such a target would be difficult in the extreme but the optimism which I carried away with me persisted to the eve of the First Test at Trent Bridge. Indeed, it did so to the moment I spun the coin outside the pavilion—and Lindsay Hassett called correctly.

I felt the ill-luck of the spin of the coin then more keenly than at any other time during the whole series. I badly wanted to win the toss; the wicket was well-nigh perfect, and at Trent Bridge that was saying much in 1953.

Unfortunately the Test was ruined by rain, but few present would forget the magnificent bowling of Alec Bedser on the second day after the Australians had resumed at 157 for three. Because of bad light on the first day only four and a half hours' play had been possible.

Rain fell in the night and next morning the ground was still wet when play was resumed. I wanted to use Alec Bedser as much as possible because the heavy damp atmosphere was ideal for him, but intermittent drizzle kept the grass moist and the bowlers had to use a towel after almost every delivery. These were not the best conditions for swing bowling.

I dearly wanted the grass to dry but the atmosphere to stay as it was. Accordingly I gave Alec only a brief spell before the interval in which period Trevor Bailey played his part nobly by keeping the runs down to a minimum.

At lunch Australia were 243 for four. During the interval the weather did exactly as I had hoped. The rain stopped, the outfield dried and the atmosphere remained as it was.

At once I gave Alec and Trevor the new ball. They tore through the remainder of the batting, the last six wickets falling for six runs and Australia being all out for 249!

Alec Bedser's analysis was seven for 55. His bowling had put England back into the game.

I am afraid we did not consolidate our position. Against

some fine fast bowling by Ray Lindwall, the batting failed and we were all out for 144—and apparently in trouble.

From the batting viewpoint the weakness was that the side contained few players who had previously played against Australia. Don Kenyon, Tom Graveney and Peter May, all newcomers, made only thirty-nine runs between them in the innings.

Previously I had felt that the team which included six front-line batsmen, backed up by Trevor Bailey, an all-rounder, could not be beaten if the luck was evenly apportioned.

Afterwards I became perturbed. I thought that if what was thought to be a powerful batting side could be bowled out so easily on a Trent Bridge Test wicket, the best in the country, England's prospects in the remaining Tests would be poor. My earlier optimism had changed quickly to pessimism.

Yet Alec Bedser again bowled nobly in the second innings, in which Australia were dismissed for 123. In this he took seven for 44 and brought his match figures to fourteen wickets for 99. Only Wilfrid Rhodes and Hedley Verity with fifteen wickets apiece had taken more wickets for either side in the previous 159 Tests between the two countries. As it was Alec had the distinction at Trent Bridge of passing the English Test record of the great Sidney Barnes (189 wickets) and to his immense pleasure the G.O.M. was one of the first to congratulate him. After that superb bowling England required only 229 to win and in ordinary circumstances I would have fancied our chances.

All went reasonably well until the end of play on the Saturday—the third day—by which time we had scored forty-two for the loss of Don Kenyon. Then came the rain and play was not resumed until two hours before the close on Tuesday the last day.

Even so I was still prepared to gamble to achieve victory but the completely dead wicket and the Australian bowling tactics ruined our chances. Reg Simpson and I were anxious to go for the runs and as soon as Lindsay Hassett brought on Jack Hill with his top-spinners, I launched into attack.

I also signalled to the dressing-room for Godfrey Evans to come in next to maintain the rate of scoring and that Denis Compton and then Johnny Wardle should follow. As soon as

I struck Jack Hill a few hefty blows, however, Lindsay Hassett took him off and replaced him with Bill Johnston, the left-hander, bowling over the wicket to a defensive field. Obviously the Australians were not prepared to try to get us out by tempting us to hit our way to victory. They were content to play for a draw—and to wait until next time.

In the circumstances we could do nothing but follow their example and Reg and I played out time. Long before the end, the teams were doing little more than going through the motions of Test cricketers—all the atmosphere of a Test match had long since departed—so had the majority of the crowd!

The Second Test was as usual played at Lord's, where in recent years the pitch nearly always has taken spin from the third day onwards.

I remembered, with misgivings, how Ramadhin and Valentine bowled England out there for 151 and 274 in 1950 and gave West Indies their first victory at Lord's. Ramadhin took eleven wickets and Valentine seven.

Bearing all this in mind a long debate ensued among the Selectors. We tried to analyse the batting failures at Nottingham. We also had to think hard about our slow bowling—a key factor in the composition of the side. We thought a leg-break bowler would do best, if we could find one. But an examination of the meagrely stocked larder showed that the best was still Freddie Brown, England's former captain, currently a selector.

I took it upon myself, as skipper, to ask Freddie whether he would like to play and to my surprise Freddie said: "Yes".

My thoughts at the end of the 1950–51 tour were that Freddie had retired from England v. Australia Test matches after having led us to victory in the last Test in Melbourne. In Australia, however, he had discarded his leg-break and achieved his success with medium-paced swingers. Could he, if needed, revert to leg-breaks—the hardest delivery of all to bowl—in a Test against Australia? If he could, his all-round efficiency would be very useful to the team. Frankly, however, Freddie's inclusion put some anxiety in my mind. I foresaw all manner of difficulties in having a former England captain, and an amateur at that, under my jurisdiction. But I need not have worried and Freddie never acted as anything but an ordinary member of the team.

That match, the second of the 1953 series, was one I shall always remember. Lord's has never been one of my 'lucky' grounds and this time everything seemed to go wrong. First a meeting of the Selectors had been inordinately long in picking the side, then a few days before the game came an attack of fibrositis in my neck and shoulder. To my acute discomfort I could scarcely move or bend without experiencing severe pain. On the first morning of the match I spent nearly four hours with a masseur who treated me before play on every subsequent day as well.

No, Lord's has not been a particularly fortunate ground for me. True, I have done fairly well there with the bat but I have also had an undue amount of injury there. Before the war I broke a finger at Lord's and also suffered a crack on my nose from a vast hit by Jim Smith—the ball went through my hands! On another occasion I received a crack on the leg there and, on another, was struck by lumbago.

A coincidence is that, apart from injury and ill-health, I never felt the same about playing at Lord's after the professionals had been moved from the dressing-room under the Press Box. In the old dressing-room, we were easily accessible to our friends. When we moved into the pavilion, visitors had to ask the attendant at the pavilion door for permission to meet us and they had to wait until we could be brought down to them.

Changes, I know, are inevitable even in simple things such as dressing-room accommodation, and, no doubt, this, which has brought amateurs and professionals more together off the field, has broken down another barrier.

A much better feeling exists nowadays between amateurs and professionals. When I started playing county cricket in 1934 we rarely saw the skipper off the field.

I am sorry to say that through the years, I looked forward to playing at Lord's with diminishing pleasure. As each new game approached there I wondered what would go wrong this time. The thought became a fixation.

To cap everything in 1953 I dropped three catches in Australia's first innings—and split a finger nail in missing one of them.

Wherever I went on that piece of Lord's turf, surrounded

by a packed crowd, the ball seemed to follow me. I just could not get out of its way. The only relief came when I dropped a catch off Ray Lindwall, split the finger nail and went into the pavilion to have it dressed!

What a day was the last! The Aussies, on top of the world in the morning with every prospect of winning, were thoroughly dejected in the evening, after having been denied their victory by Willie Watson and Trevor Bailey.

Overnight, England, who had been left 343 to get to win in seven hours, lost Kenyon, Graveney and myself for twelve runs and, when Denis Compton was out at 12.40 the next day, the position looked nearly hopeless. England were 73 for four with five hours left for play—long odds on an Australian victory, particularly as the England tail looked very weak. Then Willie Watson, playing in his first Test against Australia, and Trevor Bailey came together in one of the most stubborn stands in Test history. The Australians did everything they could to split the partnership but England's fifth wicket stand was not broken until Watson and Bailey had batted together for nearly four hours and a half, in which time they had added 163. More than once during that stand hopes were raised of a sensational England victory but that was too much to expect. As it was Watson signalized his Test debut against Australia with a memorable century and he made 109 before he was out with fifty minutes left for cricket. Trevor followed him shortly and, although Australia took one more wicket, that of Freddie Brown, England saved the day.

In fact at the finish we were only sixty-one runs short of the victory target with three wickets left.

The tension in the Australian dressing-room at the end of the day was understandable. When I went into their room I found the atmosphere so thick that I could have 'made' all sorts of shots through the air with a cricket bat—and left a lasting impression. They were most disappointed at being unable to clinch what had looked a certain win but even so they were full of admiration for Watson and Bailey.

During England's rearguard fight we were visited in the dressing-room by the Duke of Edinburgh, a devotee of cricket and exceptionally knowledgeable about the game. The England players certainly appreciated his encouragement.

Waiting about in the dressing-room at such times plays havoc with even the most dispassionate. I am thinking particularly of Freddie Brown and Alec Bedser, two lion-hearted men who look as though nothing would upset their calm approach to a situation. During the Watson-Bailey rescue stand, Freddie sat several hours in the same position on the pavilion balcony resolutely refusing to move in case he changed the luck. As he was next in, he wore his batting gloves the whole time. They also served as a shield for his finger nails which otherwise would have been in danger of being bitten down to the quick.

Alec by contrast sat in the dressing-room all day, not daring to watch the game. One moment he held a newspaper in his hands, then he put it down, then picked it up again. At the end of the day when we asked him to tell us about the particularly absorbing article he had been reading for so long, he muttered "which article?" He hadn't read a line!

When Alec wasn't going through the pretence of reading his newspaper he unpacked his bag, cleaned his boots, gave the spikes another look-over and then packed them all away again. About the only thing he did neglect to do was to paint the walls of the dressing-room. After all that nervous excitement Alec was not called upon to go out either to try to save the game for England—or to make the winning hit.

The growing tension affected me as much, but as captain, I had to steel myself in the dressing-room balcony and try to look composed. I think I managed my part reasonably well—until I saw a ball bowled to Willie Watson pitch outside his off-stump and go hurtling down the leg-side. Then I went inside the pavilion to recover from the shock!

One thing has always puzzled me about the Lord's Test. I could not understand why, when Willie Watson and Trevor Bailey had been dismissed and Freddie Brown and Godfrey Evans came together thirty-five minutes from the end, Lindsay Hassett did not bring back his fast bowlers Lindwall and Miller. Possibly Lindsay by then had decided that chances of an Australian victory had gone. If so, his readiness to accept a situation as lost was very unlike the usually astute Lindsay Hassett.

I am inclined to think that he had forgotten the M.C.C. tour of 1950–51 in which, well as he played earlier, Freddie Brown's weakness against very fast bowling was exposed from the Third Test onwards. And, after all, Freddie had been recalled, not as a batsman, but as a spin-bowler.

Not that Freddie Brown alone was likely to be uncomfortable and uncertain against Lindwall and Miller. Godfrey Evans had never been at his best against really fast bowling, and Alec Bedser and Brian Statham, like most tail-enders, always prefer to bat against slow bowlers.

Still I didn't lose any sleep in worrying over any opportunities lost by the Australians. We England selectors had enough problems of our own. The teams were still level in the rubber, which seemed to me to be a fair position at that stage, and we thought England stood a fine chance of winning at Manchester.

We had taken the strain in two Tests. Could we now begin the pull home? That was the question.

Despite the sharp division of opinion on the merits of Don Kenyon as a Test opening batsman he had retained his place for the match at Lord's, but his failures there (three and two) made me think that to that point he had not acquired the right temperament for Test cricket. Those who disagreed with me before the Lord's Test could now see things my way, and the decision was taken to bring back Bill Edrich for Manchester, a decision I particularly welcomed, as I had always admired the qualities of Bill Edrich as a cricketer.

In my view a mistake was made by not including Edrich in the M.C.C. team which toured Australia in 1950–51. I believe that with him in the side England might even have regained the Ashes then. Someone of his experience and fighting spirit might have turned the scales which, despite the four-one defeat, could so easily have tilted the other way.

However, Bill was back in the England team now and I was satisfied. Freddie Trueman was also included among the original twelve selections but was omitted from the team when we decided to rely on the three specialist bowlers, Bedser and Wardle and Laker, with Trevor Bailey to support them.

A word here about Peter May. This young Surrey amateur of such high promise had been left out of the side after the First Test at a time when most people outside the game thought

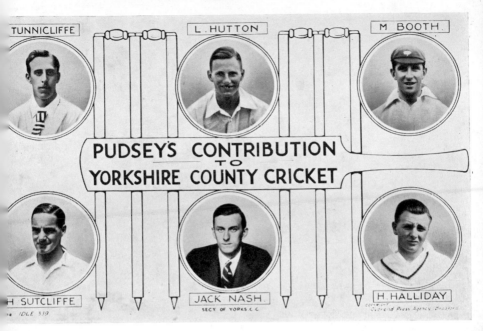

TUNNICLIFFE L. HUTTON M BOOTH.

PUDSEY'S CONTRIBUTION TO YORKSHIRE COUNTY CRICKET

H SUTCLIFFE. JACK NASH.
SECY OF YORKS C.C. H. HALLIDAY

Men of Pudsey

Eye on the ball

My first Test against Australia, Nottingham,
1938. Barnett, my companion here, and I scored
219 for the first wicket

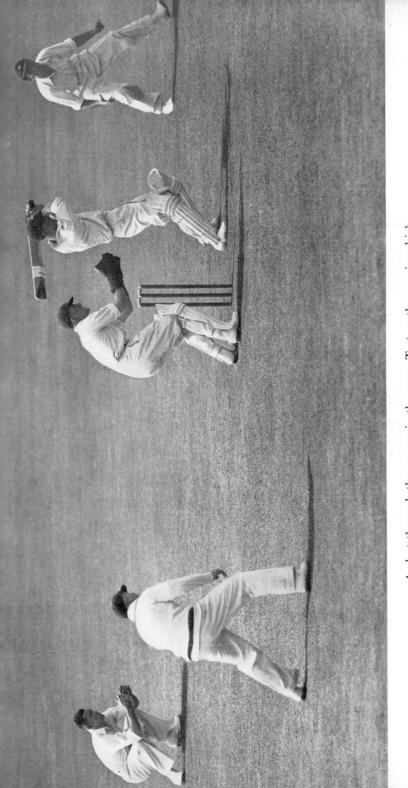

A shot through the covers in the same Test as the one in which Barnett and I scored 219 for the first wicket

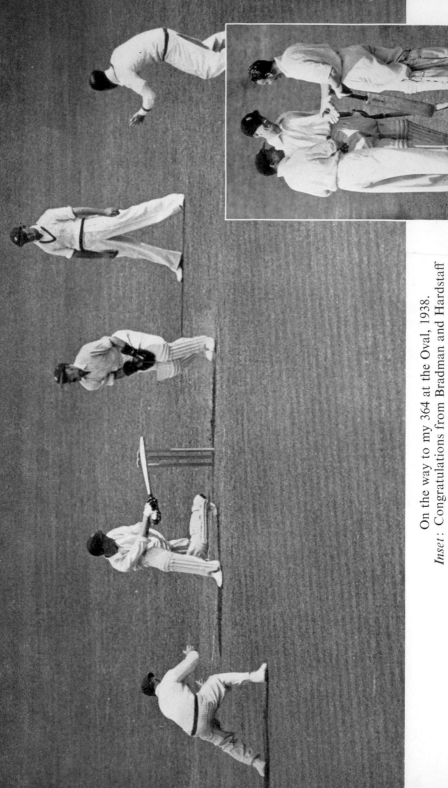

On the way to my 364 at the Oval, 1938.
Inset: Congratulations from Bradman and Hardstaff

his star would be in the ascendant. You may have been among those who wondered why. I will tell you.

Much as they were certain of his potential as a Test cricketer the Selectors felt that, as Peter had had five successive low scores against the Australians—two while playing for Surrey (o and 1), two for the m.c.c. (16 and 11) and another in the First Test (9)—they could best help him to regain confidence by resting him.

At the start of the tour the Australians fully realized that Peter was likely to be a danger to them. So, with typical Australian thoroughness, they did everything they could to destroy his confidence from the first time they played against him. Recognizing that he was on the short list of players likely to be chosen against them, they applied the technique at which they are so adept—they set out to stop the bud from flowering.

Peter's figures for his first five innings—37 runs, average 7.4—against them paid testimony to the skill with which they went to their task and after the First Test the England Selectors had to admit that the Aussies had won a temporary advantage.

The point had to be considered whether better results would be obtained by keeping Peter in the side and risking further failures which might destroy his confidence for a long time to come, or by resting him from Test cricket for a while in the hope that he would make a series of big scores in county cricket and return to Test cricket refreshed and with confidence restored.

We decided on the latter policy and, although Peter went his merry way in county cricket, we did not recall him until the last Test, on his home ground, at the Oval—a match on which the destiny of the Ashes was to depend. No one was more delighted than the Selectors when Peter played a signal part in England's victory there, and his contribution to the retention of the Ashes eighteen months later is now history.

To restrict the activities of any potential Test player they meet in county and other games is one example of the intensity of purpose the Australians bring to their cricket.

They tried similar tactics on Colin Cowdrey of Kent whom they regarded as the best young English batsman they played against in 1953. In the Gentlemen of England match at Lord's they did their utmost to dismiss him cheaply but he made fifty

c

against them in both innings and repeated his success in the next match for Kent against the Australians at Canterbury.

The Australians are just as artful at 'encouraging' batsmen they hope to see selected by allowing them to help themselves a little. I could name dozens of instances where they have done this—but, of course, England teams have not been backward in adopting similar tactics.

The Third Test at Manchester was both disastrous and sensational. Within ten minutes of the start England had lost the toss and also the services of Jim Laker, of Surrey. Fielding at square-leg, he tried to intercept a shot by Arthur Morris, slipped on the rain-sodden turf and strained a muscle in his left leg.

The attack was greatly handicapped; we had left only three recognized bowlers—Wardle, Bailey and Bedser. They had to bear the brunt of bowling throughout the first day. Fortunately for them, however, rain limited play to just over three hours in which Australia scored 151 for three. Next day Laker, who had an injection to deaden the pain in his leg, was able to bowl for the first time in the match, but he was considerably troubled by his injury and took only one wicket in Australia's innings of 318. Alec Bedser (five for 115) was England's most successful bowler.

By the close of play on the Saturday England replied with 126 for four wickets. Because of rain not a ball was bowled on Monday but things were not so gloomy for me. I was informed by the Selectors that I was to captain England for the remaining two Tests, at Leeds and the Oval. As Old Trafford has always been one of my favourite grounds, it was as good a place as any, outside Yorkshire, for me to receive such news.

Old Trafford, like most county grounds, has its character. I know one senior member who always occupies the same seat in the pavilion. Whenever I see him he is wearing a cloth cap and raincoat—he comes prepared for the worst!—and when I am playing there for Yorkshire, he always greets me this way: "Now, think on, don't stop there long today."

When I am opening for England, however, he tells me: "Tha' can stop as long as tha' likes this time, Leonard."

My three hours at the crease for sixty-six in the Manchester Test of 1953 was much shorter than I would have liked. Had

I batted another hour or so I might have helped England take the first innings lead. Instead, we finished forty-two runs behind on the afternoon of the last day, at which point there seemed no possibility of reaching a definite conclusion—at least that's what most people thought.

Because of the nature of the pitch after the heavy rain, however, I opened the second innings bowling with Alec Bedser and Jim Laker. My hopes proved right. Laker immediately was able to spin the ball sharply and he soon dismissed Arthur Morris at eight and Keith Miller at twelve. A brilliant catch in the gully by Trevor Bailey, off Alec Bedser, disposed of Lindsay Hassett at eighteen, and when Alec removed Graeme Hole's middle stump without addition to the score, claiming his hundredth wicket of the season, Australia had lost their first four men.

Even bigger sensations followed. Unable to master the turning ball, especially those from Johnny Wardle, they lost another four wickets for 17, and I think that only the drawing of stumps for the end of the match enabled them to avoid being dismissed for one of their lowest totals against England —the lowest is 36 at Edgbaston in 1902.

Some said the Australians were not trying in their second innings at Manchester. I heard that from some of the Australians themselves. They said: "Don't take any notice of our second innings. We knew we couldn't lose, so we didn't try." My answer to that was: "It wouldn't have made any difference either way; thirty-five runs was as many as you would have made in any case."

Believe me, the Australians tried hard enough. Australian cricketers don't throw wickets away, as they would have us believe, particularly in Test matches. In fact, I don't know any batsmen who throws away his wicket in a Test match—and very few who do so in any class of cricket.

Even though the Manchester Test was another draw, I thought that England's all-out effort could be of considerable moral advantage to us later. We had shown how vulnerable to spin the Australians could be.

As the time approached for the Fourth Test, at Leeds, my prospects of finding a pair of really fast bowlers virtually had disappeared. Brian Statham had not been selected for the First

Test at Nottingham because the Selectors felt that the wicket would not be helpful to his type of bowling. In the Second Test at Lord's he had bowled fairly well in sending down forty-three overs for two wickets costing him eighty-eight runs. Injury kept him out of the Third Test on his own county pitch at Old Trafford.

As for Freddie Trueman, he was still in the R.A.F. He was able to play only occasionally for Yorkshire and, though he was among the original thirteen chosen for Manchester, his lack of practice coupled with the prospects of a wet wicket had led to his omission from the eleven.

Neither Statham nor Trueman was included in the team for the Leeds Test—Statham, fit again, was twelfth man—and, as my hopes had rested largely on them as the two fast bowlers for whom I had been searching, my disappointment may be understood. Still, I had not abandoned my quest. I saw plenty of time for Trueman to make the grade, after he left the R.A.F. and returned to regular first-class cricket.

The star of these two young speed-merchants had been temporarily eclipsed, but another was about to burst in the cricket firmament, for Tony Lock, of Surrey, played his first Test against Australia at Leeds. In him, I firmly believed England had discovered the best *attacking* slow left-arm bowler since the days of Charlie Parker, of Gloucestershire. My allusion to Charlie Parker and not Hedley Verity I know, will sound like heresy in my native Yorkshire. I had better give my reasons.

In my opinion Hedley Verity, the greatest Yorkshire slow left-hander since Wilfrid Rhodes, lost a little of his ability to spin the ball on good wickets after he had been on two overseas tours. As a result he became more defensive in his approach and was inclined to bowl 'tight' and wait for the batsmen to make mistakes. By contrast, my memory of Charlie Parker is that he attacked the batsmen and sought to spin them out even on the best batting wickets—just as Tony Lock does today. Where the wickets were in any degree helpful, however, Hedley Verity never lost his guile or his mastery over batsmen. His figures to the end of his career speak for themselves.

As for Tony Lock, I was convinced he was capable, at twenty-four and in the infancy of his career, of producing a left-hander's vicious spin under all conditions. Moreover, he was gifted with the right temperament for the big occasion.

He needed it at Leeds, where he came in for the local favourite, Johnnie Wardle, on Johnnie's own 'mook 'eap', to use the Yorkshire idiom. How hard Tony tried to justify his selection! Perhaps he tried a little too hard.

Yet, even today, I stick to the view that, had Tony Lock gone into the match with the experience of only one or two Tests behind him, he might have won the game for England and enabled us to go to the Oval one up and one to play—Leeds was another drawn game. I will explain my reasons for saying that later.

Keen as I was to win the Fourth Test in my own county, I had a premonition that things would not go right for England. The team, with its obvious batting inconsistencies, suffered from an acute shortage of all-rounders. Apart from Trevor Bailey, no one looked likely to get runs as well as wickets. If only England had been blessed with such a wonderfully gifted cricketer as Keith Miller!

Injuries were the bugbear at Leeds. I sensed that, in this respect, it would be a case of Lord's all over again. It was worse this time, although I escaped any accident. In England's first innings—Lindsay Hassett chose to bowl first on a drying wicket—Reg Simpson was struck on the elbow by a rising ball from Keith Miller, Willie Watson was hit on the ankle by a full toss that went on and dislodged a bail, and Trevor Bailey twisted a knee in scrambling to regain his crease after attempting a short run. England made only 167, Ray Lindwall again being the chief architect of our failure, by taking five wickets for 54 runs.

The brunt of the bowling in Australia's first innings fell upon Alec Bedser and, with six victims, he surpassed Clarrie Grimmett's world record of 216 wickets in all Tests. His Surrey colleague, Tony Lock, who was brilliant in the field, helped by taking three catches of Alec's bowling.

Despite Alec's splendid bowling, Australia led by ninety-nine. Rain cut play to 100 minutes next day on which England scored 62 for the loss of one wicket—mine—after Bill Edrich and I had put on fifty-seven for the opening partnership, the best for England so far in the series.

Further showers reduced the cricket by two hours on the Monday, but the game went fairly well for England until Denis Compton, soon after completing fifty, was hit on the back of the hand in trying to deal with a bumper from Ray Lindwall. That began more trouble for England.

Denis was not out at the close of play that day, the fourth, but, by next morning, his hand was useless and he could not resume batting until after lunch. He stayed another twenty-five minutes in which he added a single to his overnight score of sixty. When he was out, however, England no more than sixty-eight runs in front had only four wickets left with nearly four hours to play.

Once again the situation looked black but, not for the first time, Trevor Bailey defied all the Australian efforts to dislodge him by playing one of the most famous of his many marathon defensive innings. Trevor received yeoman assistance from Jim Laker, who scored forty-eight out of fifty-seven in 114 minutes; and Tony Lock, who stayed for forty minutes in a most valuable ninth wicket stand which, although producing only fourteen runs, held up the Australian attack at a vital period.

Had either batsmen been dismissed then the Australians would have been practically assured of victory.

Trevor Bailey batted for 261 minutes for his thirty-eight runs before he was last out. Some idea of the back-to-the-wall nature of England's innings can be gathered from the fact that we batted—or rather, occupied the crease—for nine hours forty minutes over a total of 275. Our rate of scoring never rose above slow to slow-medium but preservation of wickets necessarily had to be the major consideration, especially after Denis Compton's injury.

Interesting features of our scoring were that we made sixty-two in 100 minutes on Saturday; 115 in four hours on Monday and ninety-eight in four hours on Tuesday.

After this protracted defence Australia were faced with the task of scoring 177 to win in 115 minutes.

I knew such a target was far from impossible for the Australians but I did not take the easy way out by opening with Trevor Bailey, who is an expert in bowling 'tight' as he is in presenting a barn door defence to opposing bowlers.

Instead I called upon Tony Lock to begin the attack with Alec Bedser.

This was not through any inspiration on my part, but was based on what I had seen when Alan Davidson had been bowling in the later part of England's second innings. Davidson, a somewhat similar type of bowler to Lock, made a number of balls turn sharply.

I reckon that Lock, who spins the ball much more than Davidson, could do even better and that he would be most difficult to play. I thought he might even bring off a big surprise.

Perhaps, as I said earlier, Tony tried too hard. Anyway, he did not bowl as well as I had hoped and as he has the ability to do. Maybe giving him the new ball, usually the exclusive property of the fast bowlers, had a bad psychological effect. I think that in striving so hard to spin the ball he bowled too fast, consequently too much 'into' the wicket. He would have done better to have eased his pace and flighted the ball more, as I told him at the time. But a young bowler playing in his first Test has to be treated carefully and is not always so able to heed advice on the field as one with more Test match experience. His length was uncertain and, in less than ten minutes the Australians rattled up twenty. The moment Lock stopped bowling fast and reduced his pace Lindsay Hassett chopped the ball into his wicket with twenty-seven scored.

The man getting the runs quickly, however, was Arthur Morris, who generally had experienced a lean time on the tour against Alec Bedser. As though over-anxious against Alec, he 'chanced his arm' from the start.

By altering his style, Morris scored thirty-eight runs in just over half an hour and the situation soon began to get out of hand, from England's point of view.

In the half-hour after Morris was out, Hole and Harvey put on fifty-seven runs, so that when Davidson, another hitter, came in after Harvey's dismissal, the Australians wanted sixty-six more in three-quarters of an hour. To win, they had only to keep up their previous rate of scoring.

My answer was to put on Trevor Bailey, who because of his knee injury had to that point not been used in the innings. I asked Trevor to bowl down the leg-side without the aid of a slip fieldsman, and, doing so, he helped Alec Bedser to close up the match.

Alec bowled steadily all through the innings and Trevor, in his one spell, sent down six overs for only nine runs. In consequence Australia fell far behind the clock and they finished thirty short of their target with six wickets left.

England's tactics aroused considerable criticism but this, I am afraid, was a position about which I must argue that we were only playing the Australians at their own game. After all, the Australian left-hander Bill Johnston did much the same thing against England on the last day of the First Test at Nottingham. Johnston's intention there was to keep down the runs and to do so, being a left-hander, he pitched many balls outside the leg-stump.

People who criticized my defensive policy at Leeds probably had also forgotten Ernie Toshack's bowling against England both in Australia in 1946–47 and in England in 1948. Toshack was used almost entirely as a defensive bowler except when the situation—or the wicket—allowed Bradman to set Toshack on to the attack.

I have no doubt that bowling down the leg-side is purely negative in theory and is bad for the game. I feel strongly that the time has arrived when legislation should be introduced to stop this and other types of bowling that are further reducing the tempo of the game. But, if one side employs such tactics in Test cricket, what is the other to do in similar circumstances —throw away the game?

Negative bowling of this description increased enormously after the introduction in 1946 of the rule which allowed a new ball to be used after fifty-five overs instead of the pre-war stipulation of 200 runs. At least, that is my impression from what I have seen over the past nine years.

The fifty-five-overs new-ball rule played into the hands of the Australians from its inception because at the time they had a perfectly balanced team, especially in attack. Analyse the situation. First, Australia had the world's best pair of opening bowlers in Ray Lindwall and Keith Miller. Their job, by using the twin weapons of pace and swing, was to make the first break-through of England's defences.

When that had been accomplished, Bill Johnston and

Ernie Toshack, the left-handers, were able to take over and, even if the pitch afforded them no help, at least they could restrict the rate of scoring far more than the batting side appreciated.

When further assistance was required, Bradman could always call upon Ian Johnson with his accurate off-spinners, who was also well-fitted to pin down the batsmen. This three-man second line attack was kept cleverly at work until Lindwall and Miller were refreshed. Then they would be unleashed for another attempt at a second break-through. After that, usually, only the Lion's tail was left, and usually it was a pretty limp one.

When I began playing county cricket twenty-one years ago a bowler who did not 'attack' the batsmen was rarely looked at by the England Selectors.

How well I remember Horace Fisher, a member of the Yorkshire Eleven in my early days! Horace could bowl over after over, defensively, but he was not a very penetrative bowler because he spun the ball only a fraction. Still, when he went on the 1936 tour of the West Indies with Yorkshire he 'tied-up' all the batsmen, including the great George Headley. Not long afterwards Fisher was left out of the Yorkshire side because he came to be regarded as a defensive, rather than attacking, bowler. He was considered not to fit in the general pattern of attack at a time when more regard was paid to getting out the batsmen than to bowling 'tight' and hoping that the batsmen would lose, first their patience, then their wicket.

Possibly Horace Fisher, who is still playing League cricket, might now justifiably feel he was born a few years too soon, and in the wrong country. The Australians of the post-war years would have welcomed him in their team—he was an ever better defensive bowler than Ernie Toshack.

After Trevor Bailey's bowling in the Leeds Test, adverse comments were made on our tactics in the field, but having held Australia to a draw in the game, England went to the Oval all square, won the last Test and regained the Ashes.

I don't say that the end justified the means. I do say that just as a quarrel requires at least two participants, so one side cannot afford to be magnanimous in Test cricket if their opponents are not prepared to be the same.

As the days went by and the stage was being set for the last Test, at the Oval, for which an extra day had been allotted in the hope of obtaining a decision, I was still disappointed. Not because England, so far, had failed to win a Test, but because I had been unable to get the combination I most wanted. I knew what I wanted. Getting it was another thing. We always seemed to be short of something.

By far the most important of my requirements remained the pair of opening fast bowlers I had sought so long. Despite his infrequent appearances in first-class cricket that summer, the Selectors decided that the chance should be taken then of including Freddie Trueman, but Brian Statham looked to have gone a little stale and was again omitted.

Thus I still had only one genuinely fast bowler to open the attack instead of two. As it happened, everything worked out well. Nevertheless my ambition was still to see two express bowlers opening an England attack.

A decision which of the spin-bowlers to omit from Jim Laker, Tony Lock and Johnnie Wardle, was delayed until the morning of the match. Lock and Laker were chosen, since it was thought they were likely to impart more spin on this, their own wicket.

The England players were tremendously keen for me to win the toss; more than just keen—they assured me that I would do so.

I should record a curiosity about tosses for the choice of innings in the 1953 Tests. Lindsay Hassett always called 'heads' to my spin of the coin and he was right every time.

Then we repeated the toss just off the square for the benefit of Press photographers. Lindsay Hassett still always said 'heads' and each time the coin came down the same way— except at the Oval, the tenth time I had spun the coin in the series. For the first time in the rubber the coin landed 'tails' up. But, remember, this was only a dummy throw. Still, finally, I had managed to beat Lindsay Hassett and I must have shown my partial pleasure. The England team, watching through the dressing-room window were certain I had done as they had forecast—nay instructed—and had won the toss.

When I entered the dressing-room, the players were making preparations for first innings on what looked a perfect Oval wicket. I told them to put away their pads but they believed I was trying to pull their legs. They would not accept my explanation—until they heard over the public broadcast system that Australia had won the toss—and would bat. After so much optimism, that was a big blow to the England team.

Yet, my change of luck in the dummy throw must have been a good omen. England won the match; I became the first England captain to lose the toss in all five Tests and yet win the series. England achieved a great triumph and I was a proud and delighted man to have been the leader of the successful side.

Freddie Trueman made a most impressive debut against Australia, taking four wickets for 86 in the first innings and generally bowling steadily. Having encouraged him at every step so far in his cricket career, I was pleased to have an early share in his success by catching Neil Harvey (thirty-six) off him in the first innings. But the catch was not so matter-of-fact as that.

Harvey mistimed a hook and I made a catch sprinting from short square-leg towards the boundary. As I was running a horrible split-second feeling came over me that, if I dropped it, I could easily ruin England's chance of victory. Harvey was in such superb form that the destiny of the Ashes seemed, literally, to be in my hands at that moment! On reflection, I think it was.

Freddie Trueman, Alec Bedser, Trevor Bailey, Tony Lock and Jim Laker bowled at their best and we dismissed Australia for 275 runs. One specially pleasing feature of the win was that Alec Bedser added to his long list of records as a bowler by beating the previous best in the England-Australia series of thirty-eight wickets by Maurice Tate. When he dismissed Archer, Alec made his total thirty-nine.

In England's turn we went a long way towards winning the match by scoring 306, which gave us a lead of thirty-one. My share was eighty-two but here I must reveal a personal secret. During that innings I began to wonder whether the strain of captaincy and so much cricket was beginning to tell on me. Normally, with eighty-two runs on the board, I would have considered myself well set and on the way to the big score that England needed from me if we were to consolidate our advantage; but for the first time I could remember, my concentration seemed to be slipping. This started when three balls from Bill Johnston in fairly quick succession just missed my off-stump or struck me on the pad. I am afraid I never saw one of them. Nor did I see that from Bill Johnston which bowled me soon afterwards.

At first, I could not understand what seemed to me to be an extraordinary lapse of eye and mind but the realization slowly came to me that I needed a long rest. The strain was having effect.

Still, for the moment, I had to think only about winning this vital Test match. Thanks to superb bowling in the second innings by Lock (five for 45) and Laker (four for 75) Australia were dismissed for 162 and England were left with ample time in which to get 132 to win. We reached our objective comparatively without qualms, for the loss of May and myself. The Ashes were ours at last. What a wonderful feeling for us all!

I cannot pass over the final stages of that historic Test without a word about Bill Edrich, whose cause I had so frequently championed.

In the first innings he shared an opening stand with me of thirty-seven which took the edge off the attack. In the second he went in first again and stayed till the end against bowlers who, in typical Australian fashion, fought for every inch of ground as though their lives—maybe the Ashes seemed just as important to them—depended on the issue.

Not until Lindsay Hassett went on for the last but one over, in fact, did the Australians abandon hope, and the measure of the part played by Bill Edrich was that he withstood their blistering attack for three hours and a half in scoring fifty-five not out—an innings that to me was worth more than many a century in easier circumstances. Iron nerves as well as top-class skill were needed to combat the Australian attack. And I felt very pleased that my claim for his inclusion had borne fruit.

Looking back over the 1953 season, my first conclusion was that, to retain the Ashes in Australia in 1954–55, England still had to find that elusive pair of fast bowlers. Moreover, we could not hope to repeat our success with the same players who carried us to victory this time. In particular my thoughts turned to Alec Bedser. That may sound a harsh thing to say, considering that Alec had been England's outstanding bowler every season since the war, but I believed he would not find conditions in Australia so helpful to him next time as he did there in 1950–51. He would be four years older and, for all his successes in the series, I thought I had detected the first signs of his going over the top. Still I hoped I would be wrong. So far we had no one who looked capable of becoming the man to step into his shoes.

Among the many things I did appreciate was the great help given to me by Trevor Bailey. Trevor always showed infinite capacity for rising to an occasion and he was never perturbed by spectators who might sometimes not appreciate his worth when he took a long time over his runs. Trevor's demeanour is such that the moment he senses any criticism of his self-imposed tactics he is inclined to become slower. He takes extra care that the crowd are not going to get him out. My fear was that he would stop altogether!

The influence of spectators at cricket matches, particularly Tests, is far greater than most of them appreciate. Otherwise, perhaps, they would refrain from showing their displeasure as they do so frequently.

Some batsmen are affected so much that they lose their concentration and because of that they lose their wickets. Trevor Bailey is just the opposite. You can't rile him.

Two years later in 1955 a crowd at Leeds showed some bad feeling towards a visitor for a very different reason. When Yorkshire played Surrey there, some spectators apparently could not forgive Tony Lock for the fact that he had replaced their own Johnnie Wardle in the Test team.

All the time Lock was batting he came in for barracking and, for once, I was ashamed of a Yorkshire crowd. In twenty-one years of cricket a player should grow accustomed to a good deal of criticism from the crowd, particularly in Yorkshire, but this, I thought, was going too far. Far from being disturbed, Tony batted excellently and scored fifty-five at a time when Surrey looked to be in difficulties. Just to show that other Yorkshiremen at that match also deprecated the unsporting attitude of some of the crowd, one spectator telephoned me at home that night and asked me to go along next day and congratulate Lock on his fine display. I would have done so anyway, but the telephone request made me careful not to forget.

CHAPTER III

STORM IN THE WEST INDIES

I HAVE emphasized all through that my biggest search, as captain of England, was for a pair of fast opening bowlers, and that the men I had most in mind were Brian Statham and Freddie Trueman.

From the time I took over the leadership in 1952 I estimated that two years would be needed for my plan to materialize. It took just that. These two young men, from rival counties of Red and White Roses, first came together in an England team on the M.C.C. tour to the West Indies in the early months of 1954.

Mention of Statham and Trueman is scarcely possible without reference again to Alec Bedser. As an old friend of his and one of his strongest admirers as a bowler, I was genuinely sorry that Alec chose not to go to the West Indies.

But, as captain of England, I was not so sorry. His decision to stay at home to prepare for the 1954 season eased my immediate Test team problems considerably, because I was extremely keen to try out, without embarrassment, my theories about an opening attack. And undoubtedly Alec's presence in the West Indies would have caused me considerable embarrassment had I tried to begin the experiments in which, I thought, lay the solution to England's prospects of going to Australia in the following winter with a team capable of retaining the Ashes.

No England skipper can allow sentiment to interfere with his judgment and some people closest to the game had already seen clear indication that Alec was not as deadly a bowler as before. The fact that he took thirty-nine wickets in the Tests with Australia in 1953 would seem to conflict most severely with my beliefs but, although I recognized that his control of length and swing remained of the top quality, I thought on a true wicket he did not make the ball 'hurry through' as of old.

What might have been overlooked by the statistical experts who made so much of his figures was that the conditions,

46

particularly the heavy atmosphere in England in 1953, were
very much in favour of his type of bowling.

I know I am open to criticism for making any such remark
about Alec but I can only give my honest opinion. That I do,
without in any way losing one whit of my regard for Alec either
as a bowler or as a sportsman. I place him unhesitatingly above
all medium-pace bowlers of my time, and as a sportsman—I
know of no better.

Without the atmospheric or pitch conditions we had in
England in 1953, however, I think Alec would have found
wickets far harder to get in West Indies.

Close followers of cricket may, for instance, have noticed in
the 1953 Tests that when Alec bowled on a good batting pitch
the ball no longer 'exploded' into the wicket-keeper's gloves
as it had done in earlier seasons even in similar conditions.
In other words he had lost a little of his 'fire'—a quality most
needed in the West Indies where usually the only very successful bowlers have been those of exceptional pace.

*   *   *

The exacting climate of West Indies demands the selection
of men physically able to stand up to the conditions. For that
reason a number of young batsmen were included in the side.
Moveover someone soon had to be 'blooded' for Tests against
the Australians.

I admit that, at thirty-eight, I was not a young man but I
managed to take a complete rest before the tour and I kept
fit with golf. I was anxious that the other members of the team
also should be as fit as possible and I wrote to each man,
stressing the importance of physical fitness. I knew that as we
would be flying into a tropical climate in the middle of an
English winter any surplus weight put on since the end of the
county season not only would be difficult to take off but would
add to the risk of early injury in the field.

The possibilities of illness on a cricket tour is something
which always has to be risked. Injuries, on the other hand, can
be reduced to a minimum by ensuring that the players reach
peak fitness before the tour begins. I was pleased that the M.C.C.
side arrived in the West Indies 100 per cent fit and I think

the people of the West Indies quickly realized that we meant 'business'. For my part, I believed our opponents would be extremely hard to beat. A knowledge of the conditions, especially tropical conditions, and acclimatization to heat through the years, must be a big advantage to the home team against visitors from a country with such a temperate climate as that of England.

*　　*　　*

The first mistake I made was to allow Freddie Trueman to bowl against George Headley at Innswood in the first minor match of the tour against Combined Parishes.

To appreciate my blunder, the popularity of George Headley with the Jamaican public must be understood. The Jamaicans had raised £1,000 to bring George home from England just to play against M.C.C. George was then forty-five, and he had not played against top-class fast bowling for many years.

Two or three days before the game, the M.C.C. players were practising in the nets, watched by hundreds of dark-skinned cricket-lovers of all ages. Then, twirling his bat, out strode George Headley, 'King George' as he is known to his own folk.

George took his place in one of the vacant nets and, in a flash, interest in the M.C.C. players vanished. They were deserted while the chattering crowds surged round the net where George, the island hero, was preparing for his practice knock. All the M.C.C. cricketers stopped to look at the fascinating spectacle. Every time George hit the ball hard the crowd cheered excitedly. By the way they behaved, you would have thought that, at that very moment, he was completing another of his illustrious Test centuries!

George Headley certainly captured all the limelight that day. Perhaps this tremendous fervour and the fact that the public had spent such a lot of money to bring him home to play against M.C.C. should have warned me of the need for being particularly watchful to avoid any possible incidents in which George might be concerned. It is so easy to be wise after the event.

The fact is that George was injured by a short ball—from

Appeal for Boys' Clubs—with Vicar of Leeds

Late cut

Cover drive

Freddie Trueman, of all people. The mishap was such as no one could foresee, but happen it did.

In his prime, George was one of the finest hookers I have seen in all my years of cricket. Yet I thought that he was now well past his prime. His eye was not as keen as before and his timing of the hook stroke was less accurate. That was only to be expected. Time is as relentless to a cricketer's eye and mental reaction as it is in waiting for no man.

When George received the short ball from Freddie Trueman which did the damage—NOT a bouncer, as some reports suggested—he tried to hook it in the manner which, when he was younger, had so often brought joy to the legions of his admirers throughout the world of cricket—of whom I am one. Unhappily George didn't hook it as he intended; instead, the ball struck him on the forearm.

From that moment, the crowd began to boo Trueman— and they didn't leave off doing so. Freddie immediately became Public Target Number One for the spectators.

Then we witnessed the second amazing spectacle since the resuscitation of George Headley as a first-class cricketer. Doctors rushed on to the field to attend to his arm, which, had only been bruised and temporarily numbed.

The truth on this strange chapter on George Headley is that 'The King' seemed to have been brought out of retirement from first-class cricket too late for him to have any hope of success and clearly, George had little liking for the fast balls he once hooked with such abandon. The spectators in the West Indies thought of him only as the great Headley of another era and, when he failed to connect with that short, but never dangerous ball, their minds flew only to terms of bowling hostility. They did not seem able to appreciate that George Headley might no longer be the master batsman of earlier days.

George did not play again until some ten days later, in the second M.C.C. match against Jamaica. In that he was dismissed cheaply in the first innings, caught at long-leg hooking another short ball, but in the second he made fifty-three not out.

I hope I am not being disrespectful to a man whom I regard so highly when I reveal that we deliberately treated George as gently as we dare, without making our generosity obvious to the crowd.

D

Normally this would have been a dangerous practice but this time we felt able to do it as the match was obviously heading for a draw. In no other circumstances could I have made such a gesture.

In my view it was better to preserve the memory of a great cricketer, such as he had been, than to allow him to be brought back to the scene of past glories and then shattered before the people in whose eyes he was an idol. Three days later we played the West Indies in the First Test on the nearby Sabina Park.

*   *   *

Despite the incidents in the Colony match, I felt more confidence than at the beginning of the tour. I had two reasons for such confidence—the fast bowlers were bowling well and the batsmen, having settled down to the strange conditions, were in good form. This was especially so in the case of Willie Watson, Tom Graveney and Peter May.

Shortly before the Test was to begin the West Indies captain, J. B. Stollmeyer, asked for a meeting with the M.C.C. manager, Charles Palmer, a second West Indies representative in G. E. Gomez (vice-captain) and myself. He said he hoped to reach agreement on a limitation of the number of 'bouncers' to be used in any one period of the match. Stollmeyer wanted to restrict bouncers to one an over.

I would not agree. Instead I insisted that cricket must be played according to the rules as made by M.C.C., and that any private 'agreements' were both unnecessary and foreign to the spirit of the game.

I had no intention of submitting the West Indies batsmen to intimidatory bowling. For my part I intended to conduct the game along the lines laid down by the Imperial Cricket Conference.

Unfair tactics are solely for the umpires to deal with, if and as they think necessary. In my two years of captaincy no umpire had made any approach to me concerning 'bouncing' by any of my bowlers, and I was certain none would find occasion to do so in West Indies.

England lost the First Test, by 140 runs. I felt we were unlucky. Set to get 457 in the second innings we made 130 before losing a wicket. On the small Kingston ground, with its quick outfield, the possibility of scoring even as big a number of runs as were required looked to be within our capabilities. As events turned out the task was too much but I believe the issue could so easily have gone the other way.

West Indies made 417 in their first innings and, as England scored only 170, our opponents were in a position to make us follow on. Stollmeyer looked to be afraid of our batting strength, even though we had failed to produce our best in the first innings, because he chose to bat again. This pleased few of the crowd, who thought he was being unduly apprehensive and when he walked out to begin his team's second innings he was booed all the way to the wicket—a spontaneous outburst all round the ground.

I have never seen or heard of the captain of a Test team playing at home treated in anything like this unfriendly way. Stollmeyer was so worried about the barracking that he feared that, if the West Indies lost, the crowd would get out of hand on the last day. Accordingly extra police were drafted to the ground—as it turned out, an unnecessary precaution.

To try to think of these incidents in an England setting, we should attempt to imagine Lord's with dozens of uniformed and armed policemen mingling among the crowd. Usually the only disturbers of the Lord's serenity are those pigeons who, by their frequent mass flights from one side of the ground to the other, awaken those contented gentlemen snoozing under the sun.

But sense the vastly different atmosphere in the West Indies. No wonder some of the players, and many spectators, become anxious and inclined to be rattled.

Take this for example. The wife of one of the Test umpires, Burke, was sitting in the grandstand, with her son, when they became the objects of a stream of abuse from the onlookers because of a decision made by her husband. This is what happened. After Holt had made ninety-four in the West Indies first innings, Brian Statham struck him on the pad and appealed for leg before. Up went Burke's finger. Those in the crowd who resented his decision declared they did so because Holt had been given out when six runs short of his century!

Afterwards Burke came to me and said that because of the

attack upon his wife and son he was retiring from umpiring. As he was a good umpire, I urged him to reconsider his decision; I wanted him to umpire in the Fifth Test which had also been arranged to be played in Jamaica. He agreed to continue and, I think, deserved every credit for doing so.

To go back for a moment, I, along with the rest of the England team, was most surprised when George Headley was chosen for the First Test. We knew just how much we had 'eased up' on him at Innswood but we thought the more discerning of the West Indies officials also must have realized what had happened.

When we heard of his selection for the Test we could only conclude that the West Indies Selectors were not as observant as we had expected.

However, knowing the possibility of more 'incidents' from this temperamental race of people whose partisanship might cause their enthusiasm to spill over at any moment, I decided to deal prudently with George.

On that account I instructed the England bowlers to give Headley an easy ball to allow him to get off the mark and I asked the fielders to stand back so that he could do so.

I was not following any known precedent in Test cricket when I did this.

Having been given one to get off the mark, George Headley made sixteen in the first innings, but he scored only a single in the second. We did not 'encourage' him the same way a second time. As we were 247 behind on the first innings we simply could not afford to take another risk.

Tony Lock, who had not been able to turn the ball very much, took George Headley's wicket in each innings but the match was marred for Tony when in the West Indies second innings he was no-balled once for throwing. I shall have more to say of that later.

When the West Indies were compiling 417 in the first innings the enthusiasm of the crowd was remarkable. How well I remember the Chinese firecrackers which exploded every time one of their batsmen hit a boundary. To me each bang sounded like another nail being hammered into England's coffin.

If I have any cause for regret about this Test, it was in being given out l.b.w. just before the close of the fifth day when Willie Watson and I were going along serenely and had put on 130 runs. Watson stayed and took his score next day to 116 but his effort was in vain. England were all out for 316, 141 short of the target. We were one down in the rubber.

*   *   *

By the time the M.C.C. players reached Barbados at the end of January I could see that the first part of the tour, in Jamaica, was already having its effect on the players. They were realizing something I had already learned—that a tour of the West Indies had ceased to be just a pleasant change from the English winter, with cricket and holiday going hand in hand. Instead, it had become, from the playing point of view, the hardest tour of all.

We quickly ran into more trouble in the Colony match at Bridgetown, Barbados. There Tony Lock was again no-balled for throwing, twice in three balls by the square-leg umpire Harold Walcott, uncle of Test player Clyde Walcott, and later in the day once by umpire Jordan, also standing square-leg.

Even now I am not sure whether an umpire is really within the spirit of the game in no-balling a bowler so peremptorily; he should give him previous warning. I hold that, if I were an umpire and noticed that the bowler's arm was not coming over every time in the form of a satisfactory 'bowl', I would warn him that I was dissatisfied with his delivery. I would no-ball him only if he failed to conform to my requirements after the warning.

We should bear in mind that a soccer referee rarely sends a man off the field without first warning him and I believe that umpires should act similarly when deciding upon anything so drastic as a no-ball for throwing.

In this case I would at least have said to Tony: "I don't like the way you bowl that faster ball; watch it or I shall have to take some action about it." I would do the same to a bowler dragging his foot over the crease at the moment of delivery. Warn first, act next.

The no-balling of Lock unfortunately had a big effect on him for the rest of the tour. Being no-balled for throwing three times in one day unsettled him so much that never again in the West Indies did he try to bowl his fast ball. Consequently batsmen were not compelled to be always on the look-out for it. This clearly minimized their difficulties against Lock and decreased his effectiveness.

I insist that Lock is no bigger a culprit in throwing than 'Sonny' Ramadhin. If 'Sonny' does not 'throw' his off-break he certainly 'jerks' it a good deal. So does Ian Johnson, of Australia. So do nearly all bowlers of similar type. It's a very tricky point and if I were an umpire I would be very careful about taking action unless I were convinced beyond the shadow of a doubt. What may look a 'throw' from one position can appear to be a perfectly legitimate *delivery* from another.

England lost that Second Test by 181 runs. I do not intend to speak much about the cricket because I feel that some happenings off the field were largely responsible for England's poor showing. Take one example.

One of the England team resented a detrimental reference to M.C.C. made at his table at a dinner given to entertain us and put up a spirited defence of his colleagues. He was not aware that the lady who had criticized his team-mates was one of particularly high position. He thought her remark unjustified and saw no harm in saying so.

The outcome, however, was that next day the M.C.C. manager, Charles Palmer, and I were asked to call on the Governor of Barbados, who complained about the behaviour of some of our players. Accordingly Charles Palmer and I called together the whole team and told them to be extremely cautious about everything they did and said.

The task facing the manager and me was more difficult because neither of us had noticed anything wrong with the behaviour of anyone in the side.

For their part the players asked, "What have we done wrong?" I could not tell them. I could only repeat what I had been told by the Governor. The position was not easy, especially for the first professional captain of an M.C.C. touring team. All this I am certain had a lowering effect on the team.

That was by no means the end of the M.C.C. troubles off the field. Another time in Barbados, while the M.C.C. officials and players were holding their usual Saturday night party, an

elderly woman who lived there and who claimed the acquaintance of 'important members of the M.C.C.' complained to
Charles Palmer and me that she had been pushed by two of
the M.C.C. players. When we questioned the said individuals,
however, they satisfied us that she had made a mistake. For
all that, when we took them along to see her, she upbraided
them. After lengthy discussion we convinced her that she had
erred and forthwith she invited the four of us to take a glass of
champagne with her in her room two days later.

Out of courtesy—and diplomacy—I thought the best
course was to accept her hospitality as well as her protestations
of regret. Unfortunately, however, by this time a garbled
version of the affair had circulated and some of the mud
thrown had already stuck. Many people heard of the accusa-
tions, but scarcely any, I wager, knew the lady had withdrawn
her charges and admitted her mistake.

I mention these things merely as examples of the things
that I had to contend with as captain. Believe me, something
happened in every island in the otherwise lovely West Indies.

*   *   *

Next came M.C.C.'s visit to British Guiana, a trouble-spot in
more ways than one.

Outwardly the people were pleasant, but, when we were
playing cricket, I noticed the crowd was noisier than during
the previous M.C.C. tour in 1947–48. M.C.C. won the first game,
against British Guiana, by an innings and ninety-eight runs,
but to our regret, we felt that the two umpires Kippins and
Rollox, who had been picked for the Third Test—on the
same ground—as well, were not quite of Test standard. So we
asked for new umpires to be appointed for the Test. A meeting
with West Indies officials was arranged to discuss the matter
and at this I soon became aware of the local difficulties of
making a change.

When I asked: "Who is the best umpire in British Guiana?"
I was told: "Menzies, the groundsman." To this I responded
by inquiring whether Menzies would be prepared to stand.
One of the West Indies cricket officials surprised me by saying:
"If I say he's got to stand, he *will* stand."

The possibility of bringing in an umpire from one of the other islands was discussed but the West Indies' officials pointed out that the rules for Test matches in the West Indies laid down that umpires must be drawn from the island in which the match was to be played. Further, they emphasized that asking for new umpires from another island would lead to local dissension.

I argued that I considered that only the best umpires would be good enough for Test cricket and that I did not care where they came from as long as they could do the job efficiently. My arguments were in vain. The West Indies official insisted they dare not bring umpires from outside British Guiana and they suggested approaching B. Gaskin, a local resident, who played twice for West Indies against England in 1947. To this I agreed but, when Gaskin was asked whether he would stand, he excused himself on the grounds of inexperience. Finally, L. S. Gillette, who had retired from umpiring after crowd disturbances the previous season when India played at Georgetown, and B. Menzies, the groundsman, were appointed.

From the point of view of a lack of incidents, everything worked out reasonably well until the fourth day when Menzies gave the local player, McWatt, run out when he had made fifty-four and had helped Holt put on ninety-nine runs in West Indies' first innings.

Later, when I learned that many bets had been made in the crowd on the chances of the partnership reaching 100, I began to understand how the excitement had risen to such heights when the stand was broken as the batsmen scrambled for the run which would have completed the hundred.

I thought that the decision by Menzies was right. I was in no doubt that McWatt was well out of his ground when the wicket was broken but many of the crowd began booing, and making a noise such as I have rarely heard in a cricket ground.

Yet, I was not unduly perturbed until I saw Peter May, whose smart return of the ball had ended McWatt's innings, running in from the boundary to escape a shower of bottles which were being thrown on to the ground. These were followed by wooden crates and all manner of missiles.

The look on Peter's face as he ran towards me was one I

shall never forget and for some time the scene and atmosphere were most unhealthy.

Despite all the provocation by the crowd, however, I was eager to carry on with the cricket. Suddenly I saw that Umpire Menzies was on his way to the pavilion at a fair sprint.

I shouted to our players: "Stop Menzies, don't let him get off the field." I thought that if Menzies reached the safety of the pavilion, he would stay there and no further cricket would be played that day. Apart from a determination not to allow the crowd to control the situation, I wanted to take the last two wickets as quickly as possible and force West Indies to follow-on.

England had scored 401 and at that point West Indies were 238 for eight, with just over two days left to play.

Luckily, Willie Watson was able to stop Menzies and bring him back. I immediately went over to Menzies and tried to reassure him, saying: "You have no need to be afraid of the crowd. Just stay here and do your best. We will look after you."

At that point the President of the British Guiana Cricket Association came on to the field and advised me against any more cricket that day. He said the situation was becoming explosive and dangerous. I told him I preferred to restart the game and that in order not to invite further trouble I would, if necessary, avoid playing fielders on the boundary. I added: "I want to win the match and I cannot afford to lose time by going off the field just now. The crowd are not going to get us down. We want another couple of wickets before the close."

When the game was resumed I did not send a man into the long field. Play proceeded in an atmosphere charged with electricity for the last twenty-five minutes. In that time we took one more wicket, which helped a bit towards our objective of enforcing a follow-on.

At the end of a day's play the normal procedure in a Test match is for the umpires to pocket the bails and pull up the stumps. As soon as the last ball had been bowled at Georgetown, however, I saw something unique in my experience—an umpire intent on reaching the pavilion in world-record time! Menzies did not wait to complete his duties as umpire. He left the stumps and bails to look after themselves while he sprinted towards the pavilion. I thought then that had McWatt produced such a turn of speed he might have saved his wicket and avoided the pandemonium that followed!

A guard, formed by local officials, who had gathered to protect the players and umpires, were armed with cricket stumps, sticks and all manner of other weapons. Purposely the England team refused to hurry off the field and I was proud of the way all conducted themselves.

Over the week-end police guarded Menzies' house on the ground. Suggestions were also made to us that the Army should be called in as protection for the cricketers on the Monday.

Had we wanted, British soldiers as well as the local riot squad would have been stationed round the ground, but we declined the offer. Charles Palmer and I thought that our best method of approaching the situation would be to avoid giving the impression that we had been affected, still less frightened, by the fracas.

In fairness to the Georgetown officials, I would say that they did everything possible to maintain order and they gave the M.C.C. players the fullest consideration. I appreciated that their position was far from enviable, as they had met something not previously encountered by any ruling body in the history of cricket.

Happily any precautions would have been unnecessary. Extra police were on duty at the ground on the Monday but the Army were not called in and, to everyone's satisfaction, the game proceeded quietly. England took the last West Indies wicket quickly, enforced the follow-on, bowled West Indies out for 256 in the second innings and made the seventy-three required for victory in an hour for the loss of one wicket.

Looking back on that match I would say that my innings of 169 on the first two days was one of the best I have ever played.

Yet, satisfied as I was with my play, I was always extra alert when facing 'Sonny' Ramadhin, that prince of slow bowlers. To me Ramadhin was still as interesting and fascinating to bat against as Australia's Bill O'Reilly, the greatest of all slow bowlers against whom I had played.

When I first batted against Ramadhin, in England in 1950,

I experienced extreme difficulty in picking out which was his off-spinner and which his leg-cutter. In the bright sunlight of the West Indies I found I could study Ramadhin's hand more closely than in England, where, on some of the bigger grounds, the backcloth is poor. In the West Indies I saw that Ramadhin 'pushed' more with his right arm and shoulder for his off-spinner than for his leg-cutter, and that his left shoulder moved farther back when he was about to bowl an off-break. Even with this knowledge of him, I found Ramadhin still a most puzzling bowler. I accepted his guiles as a challenge and I think I won the duel against him until he took my wicket after I had scored 169 at Georgetown. This was the first time, since I began playing against Ramadhin, that he had taken my wicket and I was proud of my previous unbeaten record against him. In England's innings of 435 Ramadhin bowled sixty-seven overs and took six wickets for 113 runs, very good figures considering the ideal conditions for batting.

Even so, I thought the bowling of Brian Statham at the beginning of West Indies' first innings still more noteworthy. I had never seen Brian bowl better than when he dismissed Worrell, Stollmeyer and Walcott for ten runs on a beautiful pitch just before lunch on the third morning. I remember in particular one ball, that which beat Stollmeyer. It swung in late, pitched on the middle stump, then went the other way and hit the top of the off. Any batsman who can play such a ball as that is either a genius—or born lucky. This was fast bowling at its best.

*   *   *

From Georgetown M.C.C. went to Grenada, then to Trinidad, where we came into contact with that run-getting paradise of the Port-of-Spain matting wicket.

I cannot recall anything so easy for batting as the Port-of-Spain pitch. Apparently since it was laid in 1934, no Test match there had reached a definite conclusion and the fourth of the 1953–54 series was no exception. Batsmen enjoyed such an advantage, indeed, that in six days, they scored 1,528 runs while only twenty-five wickets fell.

The West Indies, requiring only to draw the match to make

sure of avoiding defeat in the rubber, batted until just before lunch on the third day for 681 for eight declared, their highest score in Test cricket.

In England's turn runs flowed almost as easily, despite the fact that we had fielded until just before lunch on the third day. We made 537 of which Peter May scored 135, Denis Compton 133, Tom Graveney ninety-two, Trevor Bailey forty-six and myself forty-six. In the second innings the West Indies scored 212 before declaring for four wickets and in England's second innings, which was mainly of exhibition character, we made 98 for three. I must say this was one time when I felt very pleased to be a batsman and not a bowler.

That Trinidad matting wicket was suited to one and only one kind of bowling—the bouncer—and King, the West Indies fast bowler, did not spare his use of it. Willie Watson was hit on the elbow and Jim Laker above the right eye.

An interesting point about the matting wicket at Trinidad was that every morning before play the groundsmen took up the mat, which was made of jute, and resurfaced the mixture of clay and sand underneath. If they had not done this regularly, small ant-hills would have formed and we should have been able to talk about the bumpy pitch as well as the blinding light!

The point where the bowler's front foot met the ground was on a slightly higher level than his run-up to the wicket and, after King had been bowling on the third day, the groundsmen had to repair a spot King had worn on the wicket in his follow-through. Next morning, for some reason I could not gather, they began their repair work, which consisted of watering and rolling the mixture, later than usual and, as a result, the start of play had to be delayed three-quarters of an hour while the wet patch dried out.

From Trinidad M.C.C. returned to Jamaica and, after a few days at the millionaires' playground of Montego Bay, we went down to Kingston for the Fifth and final Test.

At one time the chances of the game being played there looked very small. After the First Test at Kingston in January, the West Indies Board of Control had called a meeting of the two sets of officials to discuss the possibility of playing the last Test in Barbados instead of at Kingston, as had been arranged.

They wanted to consider such a change of venue, because of the scenes that had occurred at Sabina Park in the First Test, especially the crowd's hostility towards the West Indies captain, Jeffrey Stollmeyer, who afterwards had threatened never to play again in Jamaica. Stollmeyer, however, changed his mind and the venue was not switched.

Understandably, the wires home to England had been buzzing with all manner of stories about the events of the tour of the West Indies. Some of these had been highly coloured, some exaggerated, some had given what I considered to be a fair picture of the situation and of the difficulties the M.C.C. players were encountering.

Nevertheless, I was rather surprised when shortly before the start of the match I received a cable from M.C.C. in London asking me to impress upon the England players to take special care not to inflame any feelings and to do everything possible to allow the match to proceed smoothly.

Obviously we would have tried to do so in any case but this request from Lord's increased my anxiety that the game should not be marred by any incident of an unpleasant nature. From the start everyone seemed to be on his best behaviour with the players in both teams doing their best to help the umpires, and the crowd showing a greater awareness than before of their responsibilities—until teatime on the third day.

I was leaving the field, having just completed my two-hundredth run to become the first England captain to score a double century abroad. This was also my highest innings of the tour and my nineteenth Test century. Then out of the blue occurred an incident which brought unhappy repercussions.

To that moment I had been exposed to a broiling sun in tropical heat for the best part of three days during which the West Indies scored 139 and while England had made nearly 400 for six or seven wickets. The heat was such that, at every interval, I hurried into the dressing-room to make a complete change of clothing and to rest before setting out into that fierce sun again.

A tea break of twenty minutes does not allow much time for a rub down and change, still less for rest and relaxation, and I was again anxious to get to the dressing-room as quickly as I could. My hope was to return to the field and continue to help England increase her lead in this vital Test, in which victory alone would enable us to share the rubber. All my thoughts were concentrated on this objective.

Through many years' experience in first-class cricket in all parts of the world, an international player learns to accept as part of the game such things as the crowd's plaudits or their stony silence. For a batsman the more embarrassing of the two is the ovation that greets him after a big innings.

When the crowd in the pavilion stands up to applaud, the incoming batsman becomes conscious of his shyness—which he is able to subdue in the battle between bat and ball—and almost involuntarily he quickens his stride and either looks straight ahead or keeps his head down.

Most cricketers who have experienced anything similar will agree with me. Unlike stage and screen stars, cricketers seldom feel thoroughly at ease at such times, and to notice any one of a sea of smiling faces becomes well-nigh impossible —besides usually being most inadvisable. The predominant thought is always to get to the dressing-room without delay. Its all too easy to stop and talk to somebody but the interest of the side must be put first.

Now, the amount of space allowed for players to get through the crowded pavilion to the dressing-room at Sabina Park, Kingston, on Test days is strictly limited. At the tea interval I was the first to try to make a passage through, having been given the usual distinction offered to a successful batsman of being first off the field.

As I passed through the crowd, I felt a tug on my arm and I heard someone say: "The Prime Minister would like to speak to you." Looking up, I saw Jamaica's Chief Minister, M:. Bustamente, who said: "Congratulations." I replied, "Thank you very much, sir." We shook hands and, after a further few seconds of pleasantries, I moved towards the dressing-room assuming that Mr. Bustamente did not wish to say anything more to me.

I had been quite a bit embarrassed about shaking hands with the tall, dignified statesman because my hands were wet with sweat, perspiration coursed down my face, and my shirt was sticking to my body. I felt I was hardly in a fit state for formal presentation. Still, I thought, as I walked into the dressing-room, it was nice of the great man to take the trouble to offer his congratulations.

For of the many statesmen I have been privileged to meet on my travels Mr. Bustamente has always stood out in my mind as one of the most interesting. Striking in looks and stature, with an impressive mass of hair swept back, he has eyes which hold you and a personality which has you hanging on his words. He is the kind of man you never forget . . . and always want to meet again.

Imagine my surprise, then, when the President of the Jamaican Cricket Association came into the England dressing-room to complain of what he termed my 'rudeness' to their Chief Minister. Apparently, somebody had arranged for a photographer to take a picture of Mr. Bustamente offering his congratulations to the England captain . . . and I had gone off before the shutters had clicked.

How, at that tense moment of the match amid the press of applauding spectators so close that they were literally breathing down our necks, I was supposed to know that a picture was to be taken, I just don't know. Nobody had bothered to tell me. Had I known, short though that tea interval was and streaming with sweat though I was, I would gladly have obliged. Because, remember this, I was desperately trying to avoid an 'incident'.

I would not suggest that my meeting with Mr. Bustamente was responsible but I did not stay long at the wicket after this somewhat disturbing break in concentration. I was out after adding only five runs.

When I got back further representations had been made to Charles Palmer and I gathered that the President of the Club required me to apologize for the incident! Frankly, why I should have been expected to do such a thing I just could not . . . and cannot to this day . . . imagine. But if peace could be achieved by a few words from me I was fully prepared to offer them. Especially to a man I admired as much as Mr. Bustamente.

So I sought him in the Pavilion and said that if I had caused any offence in any way I was profoundly sorry. He accepted my remarks, saying, however, that mine was "hardly the conduct of an English gentleman!"

I made no retort to that and leave readers to judge the whole of this 'incident' for themselves.

The day after my meeting with Mr. Bustamente, local newspapers published details of a statement supplied by him that I had apologized and that he and I were friends. Thus ended a miserable affair—that followed closely M.C.C.'s cable to ask that no feelings should be inflamed!

Even though I remain today at a loss to know why I was expected to apologize to Mr. Bustamente I think I did the right thing by doing so. If that was the best way to smooth over an awkward situation I suppose it achieved its object—without doing me any lasting harm.

Cricket has always been so much a part of my existence that it has occupied my thoughts to the exclusion of other things, particularly after I took over the captaincy of England.

I was not trained in the Diplomatic Corps to the niceties of polite conversation in the most unlikely places at the most inconvenient moments. If I erred in any way, I trust that I will be forgiven for not realizing what was required of me. At worst, it was no more than a misunderstanding between two persons whose lines of thought did not coincide—on a very hot afternoon in Kingston.

Such matters apart, England won the Test and so after being two down with two to play drew level in the rubber. In the first innings we made 414 and the West Indies, 275 behind on the innings, scored 346 in their second innings. That left England seventy-two to win, a task accomplished for the loss of Tom Graveney. It was the first time the West Indies had been beaten at Sabina Park and we were very satisfied with our achievement. We all felt that had another five Tests been about to start we should have looked upon ourselves as clear favourites as by now we thought we had the measure of the opposition and that, while we were gaining strength all the time, they were deteriorating correspondingly under our successes.

Yet, I cannot suggest that the tour of the West Indies was anywhere near as happy as any of the other cricket tours in which I had taken part, and certainly much less so than when I went to the Caribbean with the Yorkshire team before the war and with G. O. Allen's M.C.C. side in 1947–48.

Dead-bat in defence

My grip, post-war style

War-time match at Lord's

There were many reasons for my disappointment. One was the decreasing cricket activity of white people in the West Indies.

Still, while deploring that so few white people play cricket in the West Indies, and even fewer take active part in the administration of the game—my view is that the gradual exclusion of white folk is a bad thing for the future of West Indies' cricket—I thoroughly appreciated the efforts of the authorities to create and preserve smooth relations during the M.C.C. visit. Furthermore the decisions of the umpires were accepted by the majority of the players with good grace. There was one notable exception but I would not think of naming him. The main trouble was that the crowd were too partisan to bring about cricket harmony.

Here I feel I must refer, generally, to the co-operation I think umpires should receive from the players.

Any tendency on the part of cricketers to suggest, by their attitude, that the umpires have made a mistake is bad for the game. I contend that if a cricketer is good enough to play in a side, whether it be village, state, county or country, he should also be big enough to accept the ruling of the umpire in the best spirit.

Crowds everywhere would, I believe, be more considerate towards umpires if they understood more about their duties. I doubt whether players go through anything like as exacting a time as the two men whose job is to give decisions, and who remain comparatively unnoticed until attention is drawn towards them. The responsibility of the players is not to do anything to suggest to the crowd that the umpire has erred.

The longer I play cricket, the more do I realize the thanklessness of the task facing the umpire. In a first-class match, for instance, he is expected to be at the ground half an hour before the start, and by nine o'clock on each subsequent day; he must stay, if required, until half an hour after the close of play each day. From 11.30 a.m. to 6.30 p.m., or whatever the hours of play, each day, he must be on his feet and mentally alert; count the balls in an over; watch for no-balls and throwing; answer all appeals. He must keep clear of bowlers, fieldsmen and batsmen, yet always be in a position to judge run-outs, short runs, stumpings—yes, and obstructions!

E

He must concentrate on detecting the slightest snick by the batsman on either side of the wicket. Frequently, when bat and pad go together to the ball, an umpire standing twenty-two yards away has extreme difficulty in deciding whether bat or pad touched it first.

The umpire must also watch carefully for the 'bump' ball when the bat (not the ball) has hit the ground with a sound so similar that only eyesight of the keenest can determine the difference. All this goes on every time a ball is bowled. No wonder many cricketers say that when they finish playing they will take up anything—except umpiring. You can hardly blame them. Umpiring is sheer hard work for which little thanks are given and all too many brickbats thrown.

On the question of the no-balling of Tony Lock in the West Indies, I said earlier what I would do if I were umpire. That was not meant to infer that I intended to become an umpire. Frankly, I would hate the job. For those who umpire for a living, however, the task can be made easier by complete co-operation from the players. The umpire's task is thankless enough without his also having to be a white-coated detective to determine the cricketing integrity of the men playing the game.

I could cite numerous instances where neither umpire could be 100 per cent certain that a catch had been taken cleanly. In such things only one man can give the answer— the fieldsman. I insist that, whenever this happens and however important the occasion, the duty of the fieldsman is to signify at once to the batsman whether the catch was clean. The batsman should be under equal moral obligation to accept the fielder's word.

Even when everybody on the field is playing the game in the finest spirit, cricket is still so intricate that many things must depend on personal honesty and readiness to accept the other man's word.

If, for example, anyone wanted to find a game in which, while keeping to the letter of the law, he could offend the unwritten rule of its conduct he could pick on nothing easier to tackle than cricket. Just think how simple it would be for a bowler to waste time, if he so wished, by extending his run to take in any and every part of the field before he released the ball. He could run for miles, before he decided to let the ball go.

An umpire's decision should be accepted without question and without hesitation. Any player who shows disapproval does a double disservice to the game. His implied query is wrong and his gesture of dissatisfaction is always noticed by the crowd, many of whom may, as a result, become biased towards the umpire when he, in fact, may have given one of the best decisions of his life.

The root cause of criticism of umpires by outsiders is so often the displayed annoyance of a player at a decision given against him. I think I know as well as anyone that in the tension of a Test match, everything becomes so much more important than at ordinary times. The fact that every player on the field has a different outlook and temperament cannot be ignored and due allowance must be made for these.

In the stress of the moment I can appreciate that a player may do something he will regret immediately but his duty to the game which has given him so much pleasure must be to subjugate every inclination towards annoyance which may come to him. If he wishes to tell anybody of his disagreement with a decision let him wait to do so when the dressing-room door has closed behind him.

*   *   *

After my last tour of the West Indies I can only think that those islands are not an ideal place to send immature English cricketers. The atmosphere surrounding cricket matches there requires level-headedness to a degree, and some young players lack the ability to cope with the atmosphere created by crowds more noisy and excitable than those on any other ground where I have played.

Occasionally the players find incidents to laugh at outside the field of play, such as they did in Jamaica where a policeman, armed with a revolver, chased a man up—and then down —a tree into the arms of his waiting colleague.

For all that, such things as the throwing of bottles and crates are not funny and far from the ideal background for good cricket. No player can be sure whether, innocently, he may be the cause of an outbreak of crowd displeasure. The seasoned cricketer may be able to deal with these situations but for a young man of limited experience to do so is far more difficult.

For this reason I felt sorry for Freddie Trueman in the West Indies. Life for him on the tour was not easy. He retained a good deal of his Service spirit and his individual outlook on life and I confess that, as his 'guardian', I was constantly wondering about him. Sometimes I thought he almost needed a manager to himself! I know that he is naturally exuberant and he is still young but I think Freddie, at times at least, should be a little less exuberant than he has been in the past.

In my view, any bowler who bowls a ball which hits a batsman should show concern about the nature and extent of any injury. Unfortunately Freddie did not make any apparent gesture of doing so when Ferguson, of Trinidad, was struck a painful blow on the cheekbone from a no-ball by him in the Colony match which preceded the Test at Port-of-Spain. Trueman's seeming lack of concern for a man struck by his bowling displeased the crowd. Watching from a pavilion I could understand their objections, even though I knew that Freddie was probably just as sympathetic as the rest, but merely acting a part which he considered was demanded of a fast bowler. 'Fiery Freddie' he may be to thousands of English cricket spectators but, frankly, to me in the West Indies, he was something of a problem child. Born in Yorkshire, and brought up, in the cricket sense, under my own watchful eye, he became very much my 'piccaninny' in the tropics and every happening with which he was connected affected me considerably.

Still, I would like to emphasize that Trueman did not do half the things attributed to him. Here I will say no more than that I believe the best of Trueman as an England bowler is to come. I always forecast that he would require a few years to mature and in 1956 I think that the moment of his full maturity is near at hand.

*   *   *

From the playing to the social aspect of the M.C.C. tour of the West Indies is a small step. Before the M.C.C. players

arrived in the Caribbean I had an uneasy feeling that the
cricketing authorities there might already have taken umbrage
on hearing that I was trying to limit the number of cocktail
parties and organized social gatherings to which the team
would accept invitations. I imagined they would think that a
most unsociable M.C.C. side was on its way, and if they did that
may have been the principal reason for what I thought from
the start was a perceptible hardening of feeling compared
with that on the 1947–48 tour by M.C.C.

Cocktail parties have become so much a part of cricket
tours that, as skipper, I felt they had to be limited. I believed
the team could not run the risk of spoiling their cricket by
accepting too much lavish hospitality. The days when the
West Indies were weak opponents and an M.C.C. tour there
could be looked upon as a pleasure cruise had gone probably
for ever.

Before I set out I knew that the West Indies would provide
formidable opposition. My greatest desire was to beat them.
I realized we were bound to accept a certain amount of
entertainment. All I wanted was to find a happy medium.
Even now I don't know which of the tasks was harder. All the
time I was intent on trying to make clear that we did not relish
too much hospitality. But if we accepted invitations to one
cocktail party and refused them to another—on account of
our cricket commitments—we laid ourselves open to charges
of being unsociable.

My view is that just as the fixtures are arranged before a
touring team leave home, so should the off-the-field itinerary
be worked out previously. That could be done by consultations
between M.C.C. officials and the captain and manager of the
side. My opinion is that after their programme for social
activities has been drawn up nothing should be added except
of a really exceptional nature.

Teams from the Dominions do not seem to meet these
problems so acutely when they visit England. They manage
to restrict their social activities to reasonable proportions and,
as far as I know, they are thought none the worse of because
they do so.

Financial matters also caused some conflict of opinion on
the 1953–54 tour of the West Indies.

For instance, early in the tour the M.C.C. players were dissatisfied with some of the hotel accommodation and asked for better conditions. Some players had to sleep two to a single room, and the food was nowhere as good as we thought it might have been. I have always found that a cricketer's enjoyment of a tour can be influenced more by his off-the-field comfort, particularly the bedroom and the food provided him, than any other single factor. After all he plays cricket only five hours out of twenty-four in the day and rarely more than four days a week. That means that nearly 150 or 168 hours of every week are spent off the field.

His comfort or otherwise in his living quarters becomes tremendously important to him. Even the best hotels in small towns in other countries are seldom up to the standard of the top-class hotel in England. When the standard of hotels in smaller places in the Dominions is below the local best it can be very poor indeed. That does nothing to make the touring cricketers life as pleasant as is often imagined.

In spite of our protests, however, the West Indies said they could not afford to provide better accommodation for us and we had to put up with arrangements as they were until towards the end of the tour.

In the meantime we continued to press hard for improved accommodation in some places, and when the West Indies authorities found that they were certain to clear all the expenses of the tour they agreed to our requests for a change of headquarters. In my opinion, before M.C.C. undertake future tours of the West Indies they should request that all the players are to be provided with single rooms in a hotel which their representative can approve. Cricketers do not expect luxury but I think that a separate room for each player should be looked upon as a necessity. Surely this is not too much to expect?

CHAPTER IV

I PUT MY CARDS ON THE TABLE

HONOURED as I was by my appointment I found that the captaincy of England over three Test series in quick succession —against India in 1952, Australia in 1953 and on the turbulent tour of the West Indies at the end of that year—imposed on me a severe physical and mental strain.

Three weeks after my return from the West Indies my back again began to hurt me. I believe that the condition arose from an accumulation of trouble over a long period, beginning in 1941 when I broke my left arm in an Army gymnasium, and including my being dropped from the England side which played Australia at Manchester in 1948. The reason for that apparently was that the Selectors thought I showed little relish for the fast bowling of Lindwall and Miller in the Second Test at Lord's—but I shall have more to say about that later.

Strain, both physical and mental, had already left its legacy. That strain was to be increased by the controversy over the choice of captain for the tour to Australia in the winter of 1954–55—a controversy that embraced David Sheppard of Sussex, as well.

When a cricketer is not 100 per cent fit, every degree of physical stress is felt more keenly than the last and, at the same time, his mental anxiety increases. The pain in my back grew worse in 1954 soon after my return from the West Indies and, early in the season, I took mudbath treatment at Harrogate Spa. I could not play for Yorkshire in some of the early matches and generally I felt run down, and rather dispirited.

The trouble could not be eradicated quickly, or put right by methods—some of them distinctly odd—suggested by so many friends and even more strangers. One of them seriously suggested that a certain cure for all back-ailments was to hit the spot with a hammer!

Specialists confirmed what I had long suspected, that the

trouble had been building up for six or seven years. Time and proper treatment alone could be the healers. Fresh worries did nothing to help me.

*   *   *

The mudbaths at Harrogate and a few weeks of rest helped me regain much of my fitness and by the time the First Test with Pakistan at Lord's was due to begin I had played enough for Yorkshire to lead the England side. That Test was depressing for all. Atrocious weather limited play to a little more than eight hours and for three days in succession cricket was washed out, the first time such a thing had happened in a Test match at Lord's. Play, in fact, did not start until 3.45 on the fourth day.

This, their first official Test in England, must have been bitterly disappointing to the Pakistan players. Although the ball turned slowly for spin bowlers and gave only a modicum of help to the fast bowlers, Pakistan had to struggle in the first innings to score 87, in which Brian Statham took four for 18 and Johnnie Wardle four for 33.

In an attempt to force a decision, I declared when England were only thirty ahead after we had lost nine wickets, Reg Simpson being top scorer with forty, but Pakistan did much better a second time and finished ninety-one in front with seven wickets to fall.

The Test brought mixed luck to me. Fazal Mahmood, a splendid opening bowler at all times, bowled me with a lovely in-swinger the first ball he sent down to me and before I had scored—this was, of course, in keeping with my Lord's 'hoodoo'. On the other hand, after losing the toss eleven times in fourteen matches, I was successful at Lord's with a sixpence given to me by the Duke of Edinburgh during the visit made by both teams to Buckingham Palace. We were invited there to be received by the Queen because Her Majesty's visit to Lord's on the Saturday had to be cancelled on account of the appalling weather.

Four days later I went to Lord's again, to play for Yorkshire against Middlesex. By this time, I had read and heard a good deal about suggestions that David Sheppard should be asked to captain England in Australia, and that I should be relieved of the leadership so that I could 'concentrate' on my batting.

I first became aware of this proposal through a newspaper article about which I tried to be most careful not to do or say anything likely to be misconstrued. For all the consideration about my welfare that was implied I suspected that someone, somewhere, was trying to get me out of the captaincy—for what reason I did not know. It was not my business to ask. Or to comment on the situation. Naturally the possibility of any such major change in the construction of the England Test team aroused tremendous discussion. The popular newspapers were full of it. I still thought my best plan was to say nothing.

I paid much more attention to it, however, when a former England captain told me of a move in the 'inner circle', who direct the policy of the game, towards a change of leadership. He made it clear to me that I was not everybody's choice as captain for the tour to Australia.

This information made me decide to attempt to clarify the position from my point of view. That opportunity came in the Middlesex-Yorkshire match at Lord's where I visited Mr. Ronnie Aird, the M.C.C. Secretary, to go frankly into the question with him.

Anyone at that match who could not understand my poor performances with the bat—I made ten and two and was always out of touch—may now understand that I simply was unable to concentrate on the game as much as I should have liked.

Lord's, I have said, had never been one of my favourite grounds, but my indifferent play this time had nothing to do with any Lord's bogey. I am afraid the situation caused by the controversy over the captaincy was affecting me.

When I told the M.C.C. Secretary of my feelings he advised me to write a letter to the Committee and set down everything I had said to him. Accordingly I put my views in a letter to the Committee. I told them briefly that if M.C.C. wanted me to captain England in Australia, I would be most happy to accept the responsibility, as I felt I could do the job successfully.

On the other hand I said that if they preferred to consider my selection only as a player, I would be equally pleased to go and to give my fullest support to whoever else was elected captain.

Whatever had been said on the captaincy question, Mr. Aird had told me its origin had not been the headquarters of M.C.C. at Lord's. Even before I discussed the matter with him, Mr. Aird issued a statement which left that in no doubt and he confirmed his remarks when I discussed the situation with him.

Throughout all this trying business every member of the M.C.C. Committee with whom I came into contact was most understanding and I knew that M.C.C.'s decision, whatever it might be, would be inspired only by their determination to do what they considered best for English cricket. I was positive that no one at Lord's had any axe to grind as far as I was concerned.

In my opinion, no other body in the world runs cricket as efficiently as do M.C.C. and in tackling my problem the way I did I was largely influenced by realizing the uncomfortable and unpopular position in which M.C.C. might find themselves through an unhappy controversy which had given rise to the running of Gallup Polls and provocative articles in many newspapers.

I wanted M.C.C. to be spared the embarrassment of doing something they might consider right but which might be against the weight of expressed public opinion, whichever way that opinion pointed. I was sure they would not be influenced by Gallup Polls to do anything they considered would not be the best for English cricket.

I confess that my decision was not as easy to take as it may sound. Had M.C.C. appointed another captain my attitude could have been: 'I am not willing to be considered except as captain.' I could have gone on the Australian tour as a commentator for any one of a number of national newspapers and I would have been paid handsomely for doing so. I did not lack offers. I estimate I could have earned something like £10,000 by writing on the tour. But it was not as a *journalist* that I wanted to go.

I appreciate that the Press have a big assignment in the coverage of Test cricket here and overseas, and early in my career I discovered that if a news-story could be gleaned they seldom missed it. Thus I always found it better to tell the Press as much as I could so that they could get their facts right.

I believe cricket journalists should be allowed to talk freely to the players. Not only will they then be able to obtain something worth while to write about, but there will then be less chance of harm and misrepresentation than when they are denied information. I could not agree with the attitude taken by the England captain of my acquaintance who told his men on the boat going to Australia not to talk at all to the Press. That, in my opinion, was silly. I have always found that the vast majority of the Press will 'play ball' as long as those in charge of the games do not try to fob them off with half-truths —or untruths.

After the Yorkshire game at Lord's, however, the pain in my back returned and I was advised to take further treatment and to rest from several matches. I asked the County Committee to release me from several games and two days before the Selectors met to choose the side for the Second Test with Pakistan, at Nottingham, I told them I was not fit, and asked not to be considered for inclusion.

In my place the Selectors appointed David Sheppard to be captain and he retained the leadership for the Third Test at Manchester, where I was again unable to play because of my persistent back trouble.

David and I have always been the best of friends and we remain so. My first letter to him after he had taken over the captaincy from me was to wish him good luck, and I was delighted when he led England to an innings victory in the Second Test. The Third, like the First, was ruined by the weather.

Then the bottom fell out of the controversy. The first batch of names, including mine as captain, was announced for the tour to Australia. Simultaneously David Sheppard intimated he was not available because of his religious studies. I felt sympathy for David in that his name had been dragged in at all. David is a charming personality who shows not the slightest ill-will towards anyone.

In the meantime, and after my further rest, I felt better again. Returning to the Yorkshire side I played one or two long innings including one of nearly 150 against Derbyshire at Bradford. I suffered no reaction from that and felt justified in intimating to my fellow-Selectors that I was fit to return to the side. That last Test against Pakistan at the Oval was notable for two things. First, Pakistan won the match and so shared the rubber. Secondly, England introduced to Test cricket a new fast bowler in Frank Tyson.

Tyson was one of the replacements for Alec Bedser and Trevor Bailey. His inclusion in an England side for the first time was specially interesting for me, as I had had something to do with the shaping of his career.

The first time I had set eyes on Tyson was at Redcar in 1950 when he was a student at Durham University and Yorkshire were playing a one-day match on the Redcar ground for my benefit.

Tyson began the bowling to me and I was interested to see how he shaped as I had heard about him casually. My informant had mentioned that Tyson was 'quick', but that is the kind of comment every first-class cricketer hears several times a season about someone in club cricket and all too often the claims are exaggerated.

This time there could be no possibility of ignoring the description. The second ball Tyson bowled me was a full pitch which hit me with considerable force on the pad. I was so surprised by its pace that I had time only to move my bat about twelve inches when—thump! the ball struck me on the leg, and how it hurt!

It would not be true to say that Tyson bowled his way into the England team at that moment, but I believe that the incident had a profound effect on his future. Not many first-class bowlers in 1950 could hit me on the pad before I could get my bat down and that one ball caused me to pay the young bowler more than usual attention for the remainder of the match. His bowling was rather erratic but he was decidedly fast and at the end of the game, I asked him for his address for future reference.

Later, I wrote to 'Gubby' Allen whose influence at Lord's has always been considerable and who took a specially keen, almost paternal, interest in all fast bowlers—he himself was one of the best English fast bowlers between the wars. I stressed that here was a fast bowler with distinct possibilities. As Tyson, although qualified by birth to play for Lancashire—who earlier in his career had turned him down—was not attached to any first-class county at the time, I suggested he should be given the chance to play in more important cricket than that in which I had first met him.

Those people whose opinions are clouded by what I consider a misplaced sense of local patriotism may find something ironic in my trying to shape the career of someone from Yorkshire's rival county of Lancashire but in cricket the essential is to encourage all who play the game, irrespective of anything and everything else.

I have little need to say that time proved my assessment of Tyson to be right. He registered for Northamptonshire and played his first game for them against India in 1951. In his first over he took the wicket of P. Roy, and his captain, Freddie Brown, told me that before the second over began the slips and wicket-keeper had fallen back nearly five yards—he was that quick.

Tyson was qualified to play county cricket in 1953 and despite the rigours of bowling fast in continuous cricket, he made such progress that he played in his first Test for England against Pakistan at the Oval in the last Test of 1953.

In the first innings of the match Tyson took four wickets for 35 and one for 22 in the second. As against me at Redcar three years earlier, he began with an erratic first over, but when he found his length he bowled Alimuddin and Maqsood Ahmed with successive balls.

Seven of the Pakistan wickets in their first innings went to fast bowlers Tyson and Peter Loader, which was not a bad start for two young men playing together in a Test for the first time.

The other two wickets taken by bowlers fell to Brian Statham. So it was, in fact, an all-out triumph for England's speed attack, ably supported by Godfrey Evans who, in making his third catch behind the stumps, beat the world record of 130 dismissals in Test cricket set by Bert Oldfield, of Australia, generally considered by mature experts to be the best wicket-keeper in cricket history.

Apart from the first few overs of the innings England had to bat after a cloud-burst had flooded the Oval. When the pitch had dried sufficiently to allow play to continue the next day, the ball rose sharply, and, in trying to extricate themselves from a difficult situation by hitting out, England were dismissed for 130, three less than Pakistan made.

Johnny Wardle bowled cleverly in Pakistan's second innings, which ended at 164. This left England 168 to make for victory. We failed by twenty-four. Thus Pakistan became the only side to win a Test match on a first tour of England and the first side to beat England at home since South Africa won at Nottingham in 1951.

Much credit for the victory went to Fazal Mahmood who bowled magnificently throughout. In the match he took twelve wickets for 99, six for 53 in England's first innings and six for 46 in the second.

Well done, Pakistan. Well done, Fazal.

CHAPTER V

NO HOLIDAY CRUISE FOR ME

WHY were Tony Lock and Freddie Trueman omitted from the M.C.C. team chosen to tour Australia in 1954–55? The question so often posed is not difficult to answer. In the West Indies neither Lock nor Trueman had been particularly impressive. Trueman had taken nine wickets in Test matches at an average cost of forty-six runs and Lock fourteen, average cost fifty-one.

Conditions in Australia were expected to be almost identical to those in the West Indies and the Selection Committee considered Trueman and Lock hardly likely to improve on these figures.

Admittedly, Lock had been under a handicap in the West Indies after being no-balled for 'throwing'. Johnny Wardle, the other slow left-hander in the side, however, bowled the 'chinaman' very well in the Caribbean and could be expected to do the same in Australia.

Yet I was not particularly worried about spin. I argue that if the fast bowling is good enough spin usually can take care of itself. But would the fast bowling be good enough? That was the problem. The hope of the Selection Committee was that Tyson, even with only one Test behind him, would provide the ideal partner for Statham, whose bowling in the West Indies the previous winter left no doubt in the minds of anyone on the tour that he would be a key bowler in Australia. I have no idea of his figures in the West Indies. I do know that he was a greatly improved bowler of real pace and that he was always England's biggest weapon in attack.

So much rested on the shoulders of these two young bowlers that from the start I was determined to try to conserve their energy and keep them in top physical condition. Harold Dalton, the masseur appointed to accompany the M.C.C. team, was the V.I.P. in this operation. Dalton had looked after the M.C.C. side during the first and last Tests in Jamaica a few months before. We thought so highly of his work there that we would have liked to have kept him for the rest of the tour and we asked if this could be arranged. The West Indian authorities, however, rejected our request on the grounds of unwarranted additional expense and, as they had to pay the bill, we had to abide by their decision.

After the West Indies tour I stressed at Lord's my view on the importance of having a masseur with the players on all M.C.C. tours. As a result M.C.C. chose Dalton to go to Australia with the team. I was delighted at this decision, for I considered that the masseur knows the strength and weakness of the players better than anyone.

Troubles and problems which players are reluctant to mention to their skipper have a habit of emerging when they are relaxed on the massage table.

As the tour of Australia progressed, Dalton became as valuable to me as a non-playing vice-captain. Whenever I wanted to find out something about a player's physical or mental capabilities which was not obvious on the surface I consulted Dalton. Invariably he knew better than anyone. He proved an astute psychologist and welfare officer, as well as an excellent masseur.

On the first fortnight of the voyage the players did little but rest and relax. Not until the ship reached the Red Sea did we begin light training, although, even then, I was worried that this might result in damaged muscles from their jarring on hard decks.

I was more concerned on the voyage with giving the players, especially the youngsters, an idea of what they were likely to meet in Australia. In particular I tried to impress upon the fast bowlers that the ball moved little in the air, and that their main hope of early success lay in their ability to change their pace, using fielders in every conceivable way to take the wickets we wanted.

Then, I tried to prepare them for the cricket crowds in a country notable for its huge sports-stadia in which, as I told them, the noise at times would be so tremendous that it could affect their concentration on the game.

Imagine preparing to bowl to the roar of a crowd as lusty-voiced as at a packed Stamford Bridge or Highbury. Then, at

England Team *v.* Australia, Nottingham, 1948

Turning Lindwall to leg

Ikin and I cross for winning hit *v.* South Africans, Lord's, 1951

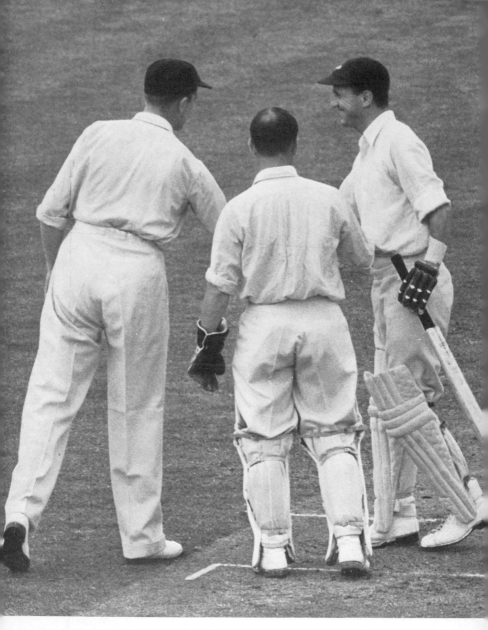

Laker and McIntyre (Surrey) say "well done" for my 100th century

the start of the bowler's run-up, a sudden hush falls over the ground broken only by the pounding of the bowler's feet. That eerie silence as he runs up after the tumult of a few minutes before can provide the most difficult hurdle of all for a new bowler from England when he faces his first Australian Test crowd.

In all ways, I tried to instil confidence into the young players not yet blooded to Australian cricket and Australian crowds. I was a little disheartened, therefore, to learn during the voyage that an ex-England captain was telling Wardle that he wouldn't spin a ball in Australia! I was well aware that neither Wardle nor Appleyard was likely to turn the ball much, but I deplored that sort of talk to my players, from people I thought should have known better. My object was to create confidence, not destroy it.

I tried to impress on all England's young players that they should do everything in their power not to lose self-control in any circumstances and to steel themselves never to allow the crowds to upset them.

Crowds at important matches take far more wickets than they are given credit for. In fact, one of the reasons for so much 'tight' bowling in big cricket today is that the bowler hopes the crowd will help him to weaken the batsmen's resolution and his concentration.

Time and again when the crowd becomes impatient at a batsman's rate of scoring, I have heard some of the fielding side say: "Keep him quiet a bit longer and the crowd will get him out."

Being as human as everyone else, most batsmen are affected by barracking, and bowlers would be out of step with the rest of their profession if they did not try to take advantage of this by doing their utmost to close up the game. Such tactics are responsible for a preponderance of just-short-of-a-length and leg-side bowling to defensive fields. This is a phase of the game I would like to see eliminated entirely, as I shall discuss more fully in a later part of this book. But suggesting ways and means of doing so is another matter. Let us return to the voyage to Australia.

To the young batsmen, untried in the conditions of a continent new to them, I emphasized the importance of forward

F

play, to cope with the greater pace of the wickets and of the ball through the air. I told the batsmen also that they would soon discover that the half-volley which could be hit in England would make contact with the bottom of the bat in Australia. The answer I emphasized was to hit further away from the pitch of the ball, allowing the ball to come up the blade slightly.

*   *   *

Unless a visiting captain is extremely lucky, some six to eight weeks are required for him to build up his Test team on the Australian tour. All touring sides there are bound to carry failures. The captain's task is to try to discover as early as possible those likely to be a success and those who are destined for an undistinguished tour. Then he is able to lay his plans accordingly. Naturally he will make mistakes but the necessity to keep the best players in match practice in a programme in which one Test follows on closely upon the one before means that he must make up his mind early and stick to his beliefs.

Here let me reflect for a moment. In my twenty-one years in cricket I can recall the names of many failures by English players who have gone to Australia—players who have been only once and others who made two tours but should not have been chosen for a second.

At M.C.C. Committee meetings at Lord's it is very difficult to say outright who is likely to be a success in Australia and who is not. Climatic conditions, the pace of the ball through the more rarified air, and, above all, the necessity for quick thinking, have to be studied.

Cricket in Australia demands quicker reflexes simply because everything, by which I principally mean the pace of the ball from hand to batsman or from bat to fieldsman, happens so much more swiftly than in England. In consequence the slow-thinker is overwhelmed. In some cases, the result is completely opposite to what is required—the batsman's 'thinking-box' goes into reverse gear instead of into top gear.

This probably helps to explain why the majority of Commonwealth batsmen visiting England have a bigger fundamental advantage than English players going to their countries.

They have perfected their technique in the more rarified atmosphere of lands enjoying abundant sunshine and clear skies. In the heavier atmosphere of England, they have more time to see, consequently to play, the ball. In other words they merely have to adjust themselves from fast to slow tempo, which is a good deal easier than the other way.

Another point to be remembered is that in Australia, the batsman with the high back-lift is likely to run into trouble. In one match early in the 1950–51 tour Ray Lindwall had said to me: "David Sheppard picks his bat up too high. I'll be through him in no time. Just watch." Lindwall then proceeded to do exactly that. First he bowled David three or four balls slightly above medium pace and then, Wham!—out went David's middle stump. That ball, almost a yorker, penetrated David's guard before he could bring down his bat from his high back-lift. But Ray had proved his point most graphically and I have never forgotten the lesson.

Other batsmen beside David Sheppard have been trapped the same way in Australia but not all were as skilful as David in being able to adjust their games to meet the situation.

As it was David decreased his back-lift against fast bowling before the tour was over and met with more success against Lindwall, Miller and the rest.

Despite the criticism of one cricket correspondent before the start of the First Test at Brisbane, when the Test series began I was satisfied that all the England players had taken as much practice as they required and I considered to be good for them.

The correspondent queried whether everything had been done since the m.c.c. arrived in Australia to minimize the weaknesses in the side which had always been obvious. He wondered whether it would go on to the field in the best possible fettle. Then, referring to the training and discipline of teams abroad, he recalled that when J. E. Cheetham's South African team halved the rubber in Australia two years earlier, the captain established a curfew, rigid rules and a curriculum including regular physical training.

I could not enter into arguments with individual opinions at the time, but I would like to state that I am opposed to compulsory physical training for cricketers for the very good reason that they use a completely different set of muscles from those which physical culture is intended to develop.

I can of course speak only generally. Some individuals may benefit from P.T., particularly men like the South Africans who play mainly week-end cricket. It is a different matter with an English player, who has to play the game for six days a week during some eighteen weeks of the year and then, possibly, go abroad on tour. English cricketers need relaxation for tired muscles, not exercise to develop other muscles not required for the game.

Keeping fit is each player's individual responsibility. Any sane captain naturally will watch every player's physical condition, and, if he notices any lack of top-line fitness, will have a few quiet but firm words with the player concerned. But to order mass P.T. for an England side on tour would be to impose unnecessary work. And nothing annoys and decreases team spirit in any organization as much as unnecessary work.

CHAPTER VI

AWAY WITH THE 'BOUNCER'

THE beginning of the tour of Australia was not unlike that in the West Indies. Once more the subject of 'bouncers' was raised since all the signs existed that the tour could, if the captains allowed, provide the biggest 'bouncing contest' in the history of cricket. The Aussies had Lindwall, Miller, Archer and others: England had Statham, Tyson, Loader and Bailey.

I tried to make clear my views on bouncers at a Press conference on board ship at Perth before disembarking in Australia. At this I was asked, among other things: "Are you prepared to regulate bouncers to one or two per over?" My answer was, "I intend to play the game as laid down in the rules of the Imperial Cricket Conference"—a reiteration of my statement a few months previously in the West Indies.

My duties as captain were plain enough to me—to play the game according to the rules as they stood. It was not my job to make new ones or break those in existence.

At that conference I said bluntly that in no way did I favour the bowling of 'bouncers'. Further, I emphasized that I had told my fast bowlers I would not support such a method of attack.

As I see the situation, and as I am sure the planners of the game intended, the primary object of the bowler should be to bowl at the stumps. I have no objection to the short-pitched ball that enables a batsman to make a stroke. The ball I *am* opposed to is that which is bowled purposely to place him in physical danger. I feel that it is wrong for batsmen to be in danger of serious injury.

How can anyone play cricket in a happy frame of mind if all the time he is batting against a Test bowler he is thinking, as I was in South Africa in 1938, 'This ball might put me in the local hospital again'?

That, I admit, was my worry for a long while after being hit on the head by a bouncer from South Africa's fast bowler,

E. Q. Davies, in the Transvaal match at Johannesburg. The ball knocked me out, I was carried off the field—out, in both senses, for the ball had dropped on to the wicket—and taken to hospital. Because of the injury I missed the First Test and I believe it was the cause of my doing comparatively poorly with the bat in that series.

I have been in numerous dressing-rooms and seen many a batsman apprehensive about going out to face a fast bowler who is bouncing the ball around the head and shoulders of the player at the crease.

It has stood out plainly to me that the men awaiting their turn to face the bouncer attack have been more than slightly anxious about their health. Few people outside the game realize the feelings of a batsman who knows he must soon go in and meet a stream of balls directed towards his eyes and ears.

Surely, enough injuries occur when cricket is played normally without adding to them by the use of these methods which are so certain to cause ill-feeling between the sides.

Moreover, I believe the majority of spectators have no wish to see the ball continually flying over the batsman's head or around his ears, or to watch him compelled to concentrate on avoiding injury instead of his primary duty, the scoring of runs.

Remember, if the fastest bowler on one team bowls 'bouncers', the opposition is likely to respond quickly and, in no time, the situation can become intolerable, with the bowlers more intent on trying to frighten the batsmen than hit the stumps.

I should hate to think any batsmen in future might have to stand up to the number of 'bouncers' Cyril Washbrook and I had to cope with during our partnerships in the 1946–47, 1950–51 series in Australia and against the Australians in England in 1948.

Someone once reported that Sir Don Bradman, when captain of Australia after the war, said he had no control over how Lindwall and Miller bowled. I can scarcely imagine that to be true, but, if it was, what a sad state of affairs! If a bowler is not bowling in the best interests of the game, he can always be handed his sweater!

Here, let me pay a tribute to Maurice Tate and Alec Bedser. Both achieved their successes *without* the use of intimidatory methods. I think that speaks for itself.

Another point on the subject is that wickets generally since the war have not been as good as before. Therefore, the pre-war reasons used to explain the bowling of 'bouncers'—that they were bowled to counteract the advantages held by batsmen on wickets so good that in ordinary circumstances bowlers stood next to no chance of getting them out—no longer holds good. Frankly I would like to see bouncers eliminated from the game, but how to bring about such elimination is a problem which baffles me. Persistent bouncers can be stopped but who can prevent a bowler sending down an occasional bouncer? The fact is that one cannot ban the *occasional* 'bouncer', simply because one cannot prove it was other than an accidental delivery. The bowler can always say: "Sorry, she slipped," as Ernest Jones of Australia was reported to have done when he bowled one which flew through Doctor Grace's beard!

I imagine that little was known in England of another aspect of the 1954 tour of Australia—the different types of balls used.

Throughout that tour the Australians provided three different grades of ball for use in two-day, State and Test matches. Now my view is that an international touring team should always be given the best ball available, regardless of what happens in the domestic cricket of the country. By special favour we were allowed to use Test match quality balls in the game against an Australian Eleven at Melbourne. That was the only match, apart from Tests, in which we did so.

The main difference between the best ball, which is hand-sewn, and the second-grade ball, which is machine-sewn, is in the size of the seam. Some of the spin-bowlers in my side complained that they could not grip the machine-stitched ball as well as the hand-sewn ball. Now, if a bowler is unhappy with the type of ball he uses he is scarcely likely to be successful; so I felt justified at Perth in asking to be given only the best grade of balls in all our matches. My request was refused on the grounds that a decision regarding three grades of ball already had been taken by the Australian Board of Cricket Control.

The m.c.c.'s team's objection to the machine-stitched ball was also based on the possibility of injuries caused by inferior quality balls. These always hurt the hand much more than the best balls, which seem to have some amount of 'give' in them. Incidentally I think the quality of the ball had no small part in the extent of injury when Jim McConnon broke his finger in the field mid-way in the tour. That injury resulted in his being out of action for the rest of the trip, and having to return home early. When the cheap cricket ball hits the bat, it also jars a batsman's hands a good deal and generally it tends to slow up the game because it does not travel so far or so fast off the bat. The only people in Australia who can be pleased about the continued use of cheap cricket balls are the bat repairers.

This decision to use different grades of ball was, I understand, passed for the sake of economy. Yet the saving over the whole of a tour could not have been more than £50—a tiny drop in the ocean of profits.

To my mind a tightening of conditions about the quality of balls is essential before the next M.C.C. tour of Australia. The Australians, like all other touring sides, are given only the best quality balls when they visit England, and no one would think of giving them anything other than grade 'A' balls wherever they play. I fail to see why M.C.C. teams cannot be afforded the same privilege, if such it is to be considered.

I think this is one case of the good workman being justified in complaining if he is provided with anything less than the best tools.

CHAPTER VII

AMBITION FULFILLED

In the early weeks of the tour of Australia in 1954–55 I began to wonder whether circumstances had brought me nearer to the fulfilment of my biggest wish as captain, to begin England's attack with a pair of express bowlers as a counter to the blasts of Lindwall and Miller.

Alec Bedser had been taken ill with shingles and Bob Appleyard, although able to play, was not fully recovered from a rib injury received when he collided with a spectator during a one-day match at Colombo. These misfortunes meant that Statham and Tyson had become England's v.i.p.'s in attack—and both were bowlers of the extreme pace. Were they to be my 'King Pair'?

So much did these two figure in my plans that I told masseur Dalton to watch them carefully to make sure they did not over-exert themselves. Dalton looked after them like a father, even coaxing them into bed early whenever he thought they were staying up later than they should.

In an early assessment of England's strength and weaknesses, I felt confident that the batting would be adequate. In Bill Edrich, Peter May, Denis Compton, Colin Cowdrey and myself we had what appeared to be a sound blend of youth and experience. In order to have as much treatment as possible on his knee, Denis was given permission to fly out and join the rest of the players who travelled by sea and, when he arrived, I wondered whether the recollections of his unhappy Test experiences in Australia in 1950–51 would have an adverse mental effect on him. I need not have worried.

I did not captain the side for the second first-class match of the tour, against a Combined Eleven at Perth. Instead I watched every ball from the pavilion and tried to advise Peter May, who led the team, all I could. I wanted him to put into practice ideas which I considered important, technically, to England's success in the forthcoming Tests.

For that reason I suggested that he should send the Com-

bined Eleven in first. I wanted to impress Australians, both at
Perth and far away on the other side of the continent, right
away with our fast bowling strength. Australia is a vast country
but cricket news there travels quickly—especially about
England fast bowlers!

I studied every ball, and at the intervals discussed with
Peter May on his course of action. As we had hoped, the fast
bowlers Statham, Tyson and Bailey struck early and M.C.C.
won by an innings and sixty-two runs. The only drawback of
such an easy victory was that, unwittingly, the fast bowlers
had deprived our batsmen of practice.

Still, the fast bowlers had struck early and we hoped they
could maintain their ascendancy over Australia's batsmen.
This determination to do everything to help the fast bowlers
gain a psychological advantage over the Australians dominated
all my tactics up to the First Test. However, we also did our
best to win all our matches. We did win the first three games.

The next three were drawn, but, all the same, up to the
First Test, no batsman of Test repute had made many runs
against M.C.C., and this included Graeme Hole and Neil
Harvey. No one had looked comfortable against Tyson; Hole,
in particular, seemed apprehensive when facing him.

The indifferent and rather nervous batting of so many of
the Australians against Tyson and Statham in the State
matches, together with the expected liveliness of the wicket on
the first day, influenced me to give Australia first innings when
I won the toss in the First Test, at Brisbane. I had the feeling
that the Australians were most unsure of themselves and I
wanted to keep them that way.

I learned later that when my elder brother, 12,000 miles
away in England, heard on the 7 a.m. news that I had sent
Australia in to bat, he muttered disgustedly: "Silly so-and-so",
switched off, and went on with his breakfast in anything but a
brotherly mood.

The chances of success for my strategy were ruined on the
first day when almost every catch offered went to ground.

The trouble began when Arthur Morris, at fifty-five was
dropped from a difficult chance off Alec Bedser. Morris
settled in again and took his score to 153. But had that chance
been taken the pattern of the game might have changed

completely. As it was, Australia made 208 for two on the first day. Looking back on this match, I count England's fielding that day as the worst in my memory.

Many half-edges also dropped just out of reach and they continued to do so all through the Australian innings until Hassett declared at 601 for eight.

England had gone into the match without Godfrey Evans, who had a high temperature. To add to our troubles, Denis Compton broke a bone in his hand when he collided with a boundary fence. From that point, Denis virtually was out of the game; true, he batted number eleven in both England innings, but his pluck alone could not save the side from defeat. We made 190 and 257.

Still, the Brisbane Test was not all loss. We made some profit as well. The most important concerned the bowling of Frank Tyson. During Australia's innings, I asked Frank Tyson to try his shorter bowling run for the first time in a match. As far back as Perth when I batted against him at net practice, I had noticed the possibilities of Tyson using a shorter run. There, with a run of only eight yards to the wicket, he had made me 'hurry' my strokes. I reasoned that, if Tyson could bowl without appreciable loss of speed from such a short run, he could keep going for longer spells than when running somewhere between twenty-two to thirty yards, and he would still be quick enough to beat even the best batsman by sheer pace.

At that stage I was intent on not upsetting his bowling in any way and I was determined to give him every chance to settle down to Australian conditions before asking him to experiment. I decided not to say anything to him about shortening his run for some weeks, at least.

Yet I was far from satisfied with Tyson's direction and his control of the ball when he bowled from his long run. I knew that one or two straight balls in a mixed over would not be sufficient against top-class Australian batsmen.

I had, however, decided to let things take their course for a while, and I did nothing until Australia were well on their way to a huge total. By then, England had everything to gain and nothing to lose by the alteration. Tyson willingly agreed to try his shorter run. From that moment, and for the remainder of the tour, he used nothing else.

The saving in Tyson's stamina was considerable. So was his improvement in accuracy and control. And, somehow, he managed to preserve almost every whit of his speed.

Tyson's co-operation was admirable. No one could have been more ready to improve himself. So the Brisbane Test after all had brought some reward. At the time I cannot think anyone expected it would be as big as it was, but we were to discover the extent very soon.

At Brisbane I also realized we had included Alec Bedser in the team too soon after his shingles.

Obviously Alec was not properly fit, and only his great courage enabled him to bowl thirty-seven overs in sub-tropical conditions. True, luck did not go his way in that chances were missed off him but, even so, I thought Alec was below his normal fitness—and, therefore, below form. Anything less than the best was not likely to be good enough.

*   *   *

For three nights before the Second Test, at Sydney, I slept badly. I was worried about Alec's future as a Test bowler, but the idea of dropping him from the England team was not easy to accept. In the event, having to drop him was the hardest decision of my cricket career.

Alec and I had travelled thousands of miles together and at all times have been the best of friends. We still are. I have always been an admirer of Alec, but I could not allow sentiment to stand in the way of England's Test prospects.

Many people failed to appreciate how much the attack of shingles sapped from Alec's strength. Even the great-hearted bowler himself could not do so. He was stiff and unable to bend easily—and was bowling no-balls far too often, a sure sign that he was not running up to the wicket as smoothly as he normally did. In this extra effort to get to the wicket, he subconsciously increased each step by an inch or two, which meant that, over the distance of his normal run-up of thirteen or fourteen strides, he went some eight or nine inches farther along his path before releasing the ball. That explained why he overstepped the crease more often than when he was bowling, as we say, within himself.

In a Test series likely to be decided, as I knew this was, by comparatively low scores, England could not afford to take chances. My view was that the combination of Statham and Tyson, fast bowlers as well as excellent fielders, the one complementary to the other, would be more effective than the alternative of a fast bowler and a medium-paced bowler, with the latter below Test standard in fielding. Thus, my ambition for England's attack to be spearheaded with a *pair* of really fast opening bowlers became fulfilled largely by circumstances.

The final decision to omit Alec was taken by the Selection Committee of whom I was only one. Yet, in choosing Godfrey Evans and Bill Edrich to join Peter May, the vice-captain, and myself on that committee, I selected players with forthright views and I appreciated their willingness to express them in committee at all times. Others may have seemed just as well qualified to serve through long experience, but I wanted men who were prepared to offer definite opinions.

Before the ultimate decision to omit Alec was made, however, I took him aside and told him he might not be included in the team for the Second Test. He understood the reasons that were behind this and knew that the considerations of the committee were directed only towards winning the match.

One other conclusion reached from England's defeat in the First Test was that five, not four, regular bowlers were needed for the remaining Tests. Bob Appleyard had regained fitness, and he and Johnny Wardle were brought in; as Godfrey Evans had also recovered, he took over the wicket-keeping from Keith Andrew, and Tom Graveney was chosen instead of Reg Simpson. Denis Compton was still unfit.

The omission of Alec meant that at last England's attack was to be opened by a combination of two fast bowlers of top speed. My hopes, starting from the time I was appointed captain of England, would be nearer fruition if these two succeeded. How well they did so is a matter of history.

Statham and Tyson were largely instrumental in England winning the Second Test by thirty-eight runs. Between them they took fifteen of the Australian wickets—Statham two for 83 and three for 45, Tyson four for 45 and six for 85. My feelings were mixed; pride at the achievements of the two young men, regret at the fade-out, temporary as it might be, of England's best bowler since the war. Naturally, the Selectors were not keen to change a winning team for the Third Test at Melbourne which followed within seven days.

Furthermore, the short interval gave Alec Bedser little time to get thoroughly fit. Yet, I knew that if one place existed in Australia where a fit Alec Bedser stood the best chance of succeeding that was Melbourne. Four years earlier he had bowled superbly in both the Second and Fifth Tests on the same ground, taking sixteen wickets for 185 runs in the two matches.

Before making the ultimate decision and announcing the team, I took Alec with me to inspect the wicket. I wanted to discover his true feelings. I formed the impression he was not over-confident of himself. We decided not to play him.

Alec Bedser emerged from the inevitable discussions surrounding his omission with much sympathy. For his sake, I was glad that he did not reach the stage where he came in for criticism because of any deterioration from his own splendid record of bowling performances. Instead, any attacks made were directed at me.

But I could not allow them to sway my judgment. I remembered only too well how Maurice Tate, Alec's great predecessor as England's medium-paced bowler, had gone out with the 1932–33 team to Australia, following a powerful Press campaign. Maurice, too, was slightly 'over the top', except in conditions best suited to him, and he experienced anything but a successful tour. Tate was not picked for any of the five Tests and, on the whole tour, he was called upon to bowl only ninety-six overs.

England won the Third Test by 128 runs and Statham and Tyson again did wonderfully well. Their bag of wickets this time was sixteen, Tyson taking five for 60 in Australia's first innings and seven for 27 in the second. England were one up in the series. The scores were: England 191 and 279, Australia 231 and 111. The result virtually meant that Alec Bedser could not hope to regain his place in the England side in Australia.

At this point I feel I should relate a story about another fast bowler, Keith Miller, a remarkable man whom I regard as the foremost cricket personality of my time.

Before the Third Test Miller complained of having a sore knee. He told me he did not think he would be able to bowl in the match and that he was even doubtful whether he could play. Not only was Miller included in the Australian team but he bowled right up to lunch time, taking three wickets for 5 runs in nine overs, eight of them maidens.

Keith showed his mettle again in the Fourth Test, at Adelaide, where England required less than 100 to win and to make sure of retaining the Ashes. On an easy-paced pitch, he bowled at a speed that was magnificent to watch but uncomfortable to bat against.

In the second innings he dismissed Bill Edrich, Colin Cowdrey and myself very cheaply before England won by five wickets. The details: Australia, 323 and 111, England 341 and 97 for five wickets.

At the start of Australia's second innings at Adelaide, Appleyard took three wickets for 13 runs just before the close of play on the fourth day. Next morning the almost unanimous forecast was that Appleyard would be the bowler to finish off the innings.

Admittedly, to the onlooker, the state of the wicket may have suggested that Appleyard *was* the most likely bowler to do this, but I knew that there was little wrong with the wicket. I had thought that on the previous evening the ball had run kindly for Appleyard, and I doubted whether it would be quite so charitable again next morning.

Had I accepted the advice so freely offered from outside, I would have resumed the attack with him. Instead, I preferred to adopt the normal procedure of starting with my fast bowlers, because I hold that, at the beginning of an innings, or of a day's play, batsmen are always more vulnerable against speed than after they have seen the ball for a time. I hoped to prevent the Australians from playing themselves in, and in this I succeeded. Once again Statham and Tyson did all that was required of them, taking six of the last seven wickets. There was no need to call on Appleyard in the circumstances.

England had retained the Ashes, but I am afraid I could not enjoy the celebrations very much as I was mentally and physically too tired.

*   *   *

The failure of Bill Edrich in Australia was a mystery as well as a disappointment to many of us. I thought that, in all his first five innings in Australia, he had received an extra good ball which might have beaten anyone, and that therefore, he had been decidedly unlucky. After these failures his confidence, understandably, was shaken. I felt that, given a fair share of luck, Bill would make a come-back. Things did not work out that way and his batting declined until the Selection Committee, of whom he was one, had to leave him out of the side for the last Test.

To that point Edrich had scored 180 runs in eight Test innings for an average of 22.50, figures which suggest he had a disappointing tour. He did, but figures do not always tell the full story. They do not, for instance, show that, by staying at the crease for an hour or more, Edrich frequently took the edge off the bowling.

*   *   *

Much of the playing time of the Fifth Test at Sydney was lost because of rain and the match was drawn, England had scored 371 for seven declared and the Australians, who had to follow on, 221 and 118 for six.

*   *   *

Apart from the excitement resulting from a close and fluctuating series the tour was so devoid of 'incident' that the only matter worthy of mention is the strange story of the wicket during the Third Test, at Melbourne. The ground was as hard as a rock when I saw it on the Saturday morning, the second day, and I remarked to the regular groundsman: "This wicket won't last another three days. It is so dry." He suggested that two days would be the maximum!

On Monday morning, when the England players walked on to the ground they found mud clinging to the studs of their boots.

I think that the suggestion that water had seeped through the earth from the River Yarra can be discounted, though this was not so fatuous as the one which attributed the condition to early morning dew. The sun blazed down all day Sunday and there was *no* dew next morning. Altogether this was a strange affair and one entirely without precedent in my three tours of Australia.

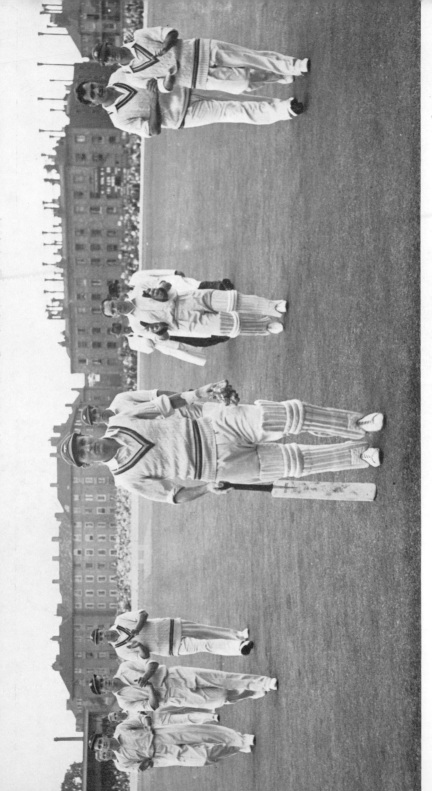

Surrey players head the applause at the close of my 100th century

"Obstructed the field—out" v. South Africa, Oval, 1951

CHAPTER VIII

GREAT BATSMEN OF THE FUTURE

THROUGH these last chapters I have dwelt on the search for fast bowlers, a search which culminated in the triumphs of Statham and Tyson at Sydney, Melbourne and Adelaide. But, of course, somebody had to make the runs—and it has been England's batting which has let her down more often than her bowling since the war.

Well, we got the runs in Australia—and what was still more satisfactory we got a great deal of them through two young men who are going to be the bulwark of England batting in the years to come.

There were, I think, two main surprises in the original team for Australia—the appointment of Peter May as vice-captain and the inclusion in the team of Colin Cowdrey. Both choices turned out to be great successes.

Peter was of tremendous help to me as vice-captain and he came into his own as a batsman of the highest class. He is, in my opinion, the best young batsman we have had since the war.

Peter had not had a particularly successful tour in the West Indies and many rather short-sighted people were disappointed in his batting there. But he came back a 25 per cent better player. The quicker pitches and tough innings he had to play under conditions which made concentration extremely difficult gave him precious experience and he returned home more mature in his play and with a much increased knowledge of the game.

I did not spare him. At times, indeed, I wondered if I was too hard on him. But his great promise and probabilities were there for the observant to see and I am sure that criticism straight from the shoulder will more often than not help the youngster, with ability, over the threshold.

Peter is a good listener, which is highly important, one of the most important assets of any young cricketer. He is certain to become a good talker. How pleased my old friend, that great cricketer, George Geary, must have been in the progress Peter has made; and how fortunate I was, too, in having him alongside me in the fight to retain the Ashes.

The first time I saw Colin Cowdrey I was very forcibly struck by the quickness with which he saw the ball after it left the bowler's hand. I suppose most people will assume that all top-class batsmen see the ball early. That is probably true but some players see it a fraction earlier still and these fortunate beings are the great batsmen of the game.

Cowdrey sees the ball quicker than any English batsman since Hammond. His bat is as straight as anyone could wish. What I did not know about when he was selected for Australia was his temperament.

How, I wondered, was this young man, at twenty-one the 'baby' of the team, going to react to the helpful or otherwise suggestions of the great crowds of Melbourne and Sydney? Sixty thousand people can make a lot of noise.

As it turned out, Colin seemed able to shut his ears to every noise while he was at the crease and played as serenely as if on one of the lovely grounds of Kent. It was said that the only thing which could disturb his concentration was the smell or mention of food, which is something in which he is deeply interested. He is indeed as impressive at the table as he is at the crease.

Provided he suffers no pain or discomfort from a recurrence of foot trouble, Colin has an assured future as a Test cricketer. At the moment he stands out as one of the discoveries of this generation with his greatest days still to come.

* * *

The team sailed from Tilbury without Denis Compton. Together with many others I wondered if Denis would see cricket in Australia again. The news of his departure from London Airport a month later came as a bottle of champagne to me. His knee had evidently responded to treatment. With careful handling he could be a great source of strength to the team.

Denis arrived in Adelaide to join the team two or three

days before the South Australian match. One of my friends of the Press came to see me to suggest that Denis ought not to play in this match so soon after flying half-way round the world. Furthermore he had been involved in a crash-landing at Karachi which was enough to upset the most intrepid traveller.

I was keen to have him in the team against South Australia, but if he had been anyone else I might not have risked him. Denis, however, is not the type who likes to be hanging around having net practice day after day. He prefers to be out in the middle where, of course, the best practice is to be obtained.

After a consultation with Denis, who wanted to play very much himself, I included him in the side and had the great pleasure of seeing him score a century. His form looked so good that we were all filled with confidence for the battles that lay ahead.

His collision with the fence at Brisbane thirty-five minutes after the start of the First Test match changed the whole tour from Denis's point of view. Had this not happened I'm sure he would have enjoyed his most successful tour Down Under. As it was, he played some fine innings and was one of the batting successes of the tour.

*   *   *

It was pleasant seeing an old contemporary like Denis playing a big part in our success; and it is pleasant to be able to pay my tribute here to another well-tried colleague in Godfrey Evans.

In the ten years which have covered his Test career he has put up a powerful performance and taken his place among the great wicket-keepers of all time. He is an immense asset to a Test side. The bowlers have unlimited confidence in him. No one knows when he will leap round the wicket to break a stubborn partnership by picking up a catch which, with any other wicket-keeper, would scarcely have been considered a chance.

His vitality, interest and drive have been of great value to me as captain and indeed to English cricket of the last decade.

*   *   *

I cannot leave the subject of the 1954–55 Australian tour without saying how extremely lucky I was to have Mr. Geoffrey Howard as manager. Though he had not been to Australia before, he had had experience of tours abroad and knew exactly where it was possible to relieve a captain's burden.

I have already mentioned the help given me by the masseur, Harold Dalton. No less valuable was our scorer and baggage-man, the former Lancashire and England wicket-keeper, George Duckworth. With his wide experience of Test cricket he was able to give me excellent advice on how things looked 'from the ringside'. As captain, I found difficulty at times in getting an over-all picture of the situation. I could always rely on George for information. He knew most of the answers to my problems.

CHAPTER IX

ENGLAND'S TEST PROSPECTS

DURING Australia's successful tour of the West Indies in 1955 their captain, Ian Johnson, declared that they would regain the Ashes from England in 1956. One reason he gave for making this prediction was that his batsmen had changed their methods and were playing with their bats much straighter. Subsequently, the Australians did better in the West Indies than any previous touring side there—and won the Test series 3-0—yet I cannot agree either with Ian's reasoning or his conclusions.

I was not in the West Indies to see the extent of the change in the Australian batting technique. I accept their captain's word on the transformation and I can understand his confidence; but I would make one or two points which should bolster England's morale!

To concentrate on playing with a straighter bat in the perfect conditions of the West Indies against bowlers of less than top-pace who are unable, because of the atmospheric conditions, to swing much or for very long or to make the ball lift at uneven height is one thing; to do so in England, against men of the speed of Frank Tyson, Brian Statham and Freddie Trueman, is another. Conditions in England generally are more helpful to swing and variation of lift and the batsmen cannot see the ball so early in flight.

In my opinion, England's fast attack will be as effective in 1956 as when we retained the Ashes in Australia in 1954-55. When Tyson, Statham—yes, and Trueman—are fully fit and in top form, they can be countered only by batsmen who observe the fundamental principles of playing up and down the line of the ball's flight—and doing so *naturally*.

I maintain that a batsman who, for years, has picked up the bat in the direction of third man and brought it down towards mid-on, as some Australians do, has formed so deep-rooted a habit of playing across the line of the ball's flight, I do not believe that he can alter his ways as easily as Ian Johnson's statement suggests was done in the Caribbean.

Incorrect habits in batting can be put right in the 'teens far more simply than at the age of twenty-five or so. By then a batsman, particularly a Test player, is set in his ways.

I may be a sceptic but, until I see it done, I shall not believe that the Australian batsmen whom I know so well have been able to adjust their methods so much that they can meet England's fast attack with bats coming down in a straight line. Unless someone of exceptional gifts has been discovered like Bradman, McCabe or Archie Jackson, I shall be far from pessimistic about England's chances.

You will notice I mentioned Freddie Trueman, who did not go to Australia on the last tour. As I have said earlier, I am convinced his best is yet to come. Whether he succeeds is up to him. I am sure he has the ability to do so. No one could be more anxious that I am to see him fulfil his abundant promise and justify all the high hopes held of him.

While Australia are beset with an opening batting problem, which was made more acute during the winter by the retirement of Arthur Morris, England's is no less pressing. It is a curious thing that England has seldom had a settled opening pair of batsmen at the same time as two exceptional fast bowlers.

Jack Hobbs and Herbert Sucliffe dominated the 1920's as the greatest first-wicket pair in the history of Test cricket. Yet not until the twilight of their partnership did England possess the fast bowlers to work in harness with them.

Then came the Larwood-Voce era, which coincided with the retirement of Hobbs and a variety of experiments to find a suitable partner for Sutcliffe. Fast bowlers remained the striking force up to the 1936–37 tour but England was still searching for a successor to Sutcliffe then.

Immediately after the Second World War, when Cyril Washbrook and I were England's regular opening pair, England searched everywhere for fast bowlers, in the hope of countering the Australian tempests of Lindwall and Miller. The wheel turned full circle when, after the Hutton-Washbrook partnership was broken, fast bowlers began to come to the fore again. Now, once more, England has the bowlers, but has to look for the opening batsmen.

Opening a Test match innings is a specialized job. Practice and experience there are essential before full proficiency can be acquired. Many of the experiments of taking a player from the middle of the batting order and sending him in first have had to be short-term policies, unless the batsman has had the *essential* qualities to justify such a big switch. When he has all these essential qualities, I believe he should be encouraged, even almost persuaded, to go in first.

I think England has two such men, able to counter the swinging ball, play the dead-bat stroke and yet punish the bad ball. I think they would make an ideal opening pair. They are Peter May and Colin Cowdrey. I know I am on thorny ground because the one big obstacle is that so far neither has been keen to go in first. In fact, both have intimated that they much prefer to bat lower in the order.

In the West Indies I experimented by sending in May to open in the colony match in Trinidad. Earlier I had asked him if he would like to try going in first and was pleased when he said he would.

I was sorry when Peter was out for a duck in the first, innings at Trinidad and made only four in the second. Afterwards he said he would rather return to his usual position at number three. As I have never forced a player to do anything against his wish, I abandoned the experiment, but regretted that he did not give himself a longer trial at going in first because my opinion that Peter would make an ideal opening batsman remained unaltered. He has the basic skill to do so, and just as important, he has the right temperament. Experience of going in first regularly is all that he needs.

Colin Cowdrey's initiation as an opening batsman with the M.C.C. touring side in Australia was also in a minor game. Colin plays very straight and has all the requirements of a top-class opening batsman but, like Peter, he prefers a later place in the order. I respect his views but all the same I still hope to see the two of them walking out together to open for England. Maybe they will give the idea another trial by going in first for a few matches with their counties. I believe that in the long run both would enjoy the responsibility and the opportunity offered to an opening batsman, and that England's batting strength would rise accordingly.

My great belief is that a good start to an innings is more than half the battle. I would rather see the board showing England 50 for nought after an hour and a half than 60 for three in three-quarters of an hour. And I think Peter and Colin would give England more good starts than bad. Numbers three, four, five—if they are good enough—almost invariably do better when following a reasonable opening stand than when they have to go in and try first to draw the fangs of bowlers feeling on top of the world before their thoughts can turn to building a big total.

The subject of temperament is constantly recurring. I have known cricketers who stood head and shoulders above everyone else at net practice, but rarely were able to do themselves justice in a match. Their mental approach to the game was unequal to their natural physical talents.

A cricketer's temperament is unknown until he has had the opportunity to prove himself. Some players become very nervous in Test cricket, others are inspired by the crowd, the atmosphere and the great challenge offered.

I bring the subject of temperament up here because it has played such a large part in the career of Trevor Bailey. In county matches for Essex, Trevor is a good all-rounder, not very much above the general run of players. When he plays in a Test match he has a quite remarkable flair for playing above himself. His temperament has served England well in the past and will do so again in the future.

I think that another near-certainty for inclusion against Australia this summer is Willie Watson, of Yorkshire, although not as an opening batsman. Willie does not mind where he is asked to go in but, in my view, opening the innings is not his best position. Having watched him closely and partnered him in the middle, I hold that his natural game is that of a forceful, attacking batsman and, as such, by the nature of things, he is susceptible to the new-ball attack. I think Watson's best position is number five.

So there we have the nucleus of my England team for 1956. May and Cowdrey as opening batsmen—sorry Peter, sorry Colin, but that is what I think—Bailey as the all-rounder,

Watson as number five and Tyson and Statham (Trueman in reserve) as the fast bowlers.

Godfrey Evans will, I am certain, continue to be an automatic choice for wicket-keeper. If he is not available I think the vote should go to Arthur McIntyre, of Surrey, who is undoubtedly England's next best wicket-keeper.

I should not look beyond Laker, Lock and Wardle for the spin bowlers, though whether two or all three would be required would depend on the wicket at each ground.

So far so good. But, having nominated May and Cowdrey to open the batting, I must attempt to fill the vacancies which they leave at numbers three and four.

Uncertainty must shroud the Test match future of Denis Compton until his right knee has been thoroughly tried to see if it will stand the strain of five-day matches. He remains as essential as ever to an England side and I am afraid that, if he were not available, the Selectors might find the elevation of May and Cowdrey had merely given them a new set of problems with which to wrestle. But I think England would more easily find capable numbers three and four to follow a good start than they could find capable numbers one and two—May and Cowdrey apart—to give them that start.

Possible candidates are left-handers Peter Richardson of Worcestershire and Brian Close of Yorkshire, who, I am pleased to see, did well in Pakistan. Then there is Ken Barrington, of Surrey, who, it will be remembered, played in the first two Tests against South Africa in 1955.

Many think highly of Arthur Milton of Gloucestershire, and I have seen him play extremely well. But he does give the impression, perhaps a false one, that he does not apply himself assiduously enough to the task of becoming a Test player. First-class cricket is a tough job and Test cricket is even tougher. If Milton finds the will to match his undoubted talents he must stand every chance of rising to the Test ranks.

In the same category, I think, is Jim Parks of Sussex, a young man of undoubted talents, even brilliance, who needs only to set his mind on wiping out one or two defects in technique to have a good chance of bridging the gap to Test cricket.

These are just a few of the more likely-looking young batsmen I have seen. It might well fall to two of them to go into the remaining places.

While I am on the subject of young cricketers of promise, I should like to mention one other, who has made giant strides recently—Fred Titmus, of Middlesex. From all I have seen, this young man will not fail for lack of determination or hard work. His record in 1955 of 190-odd wickets, over 1,100 runs and some thirty catches was remarkable. If he keeps on trying and learning, he could well become a most valuable England all-rounder.

*   *   *

Picking a Test team, of course, involves much more than choosing the top six batsmen in the averages, the first four bowlers and the most successful wicket-keeper. Apart from temperament, the selectors have to consider how batsmen and bowlers, especially the bowlers, will shape on various grounds.

The fact that a bowler averages five wickets an innings on wet pitches in county matches does not guarantee that he will be a big success in Tests, in which usually the batting is better and the pitches easier.

Furthermore, a batsman may score many runs against fast bowlers but fail against the spinners, or vice-versa. If the opposing attack is likely to contain the type of bowling which will pin-point a weakness in his play, his chances of making a big score are negligible.

Fielding also plays an important part in selection, and I am thinking of this not simply in terms of individuals. Every player in a Test team must be able to fit into a pattern. It is imperative for the selectors to choose slip specialists, a first-class cover-point and outfielders who can run quickly, catch safely and throw accurately. England cannot afford to 'carry' a player whose fielding is not up to standard.

In my long experience Australia has generally held an advantage over England through being the better fielding side. The average age of Australian Test players is lower and, perhaps because of the Australian climate, they have a more athletic physique.

Now, however, I think England can be more than a match

for the Australians in fielding. May, Cowdrey, Statham, Tyson, Trueman, Lock, Close and Barrington are young players who have all shown their abilities in the field and Trevor Bailey is still a fine catcher of a ball anywhere.

Batting, bowling, fielding. One thing remains—captaincy. Peter May captained the side which won the rubber against South Africa in England in 1955 and no doubt he will continue to lead England for a considerable time.

From the time he won a place in the England side in 1951, Peter has impressed me by the way he has sought advice from older and more experienced players. Even when he became England captain, he did not presume to know as much about cricket as those who had been in the game longer. He sought their counsel, studied it and then made his own decisions. That is a sure way to the top in cricket and Peter, making the most of his great ability, has got there.

Good luck, Peter. Hold on to those Ashes.

CHAPTER X

THE ARM OF DESTINY

MANY times I have heard that 'bad wickets make bad batsmen'.

I am a great believer in good wickets, especially for youngsters. Bad wickets, obviously, do not breed the confidence that is so important to those learning the game. Nevertheless, I learned my cricket on poor wickets, that is to say poor practice pitches, where the ball did many strange things—most of them not intended by the bowler!

However bad the wicket I treated net practice with the utmost seriousness, believing that only a fool would waste such valuable time. And I believe that on those under-prepared practice pitches I developed my ability to play well in conditions favouring the bowler.

Bad-wicket batting, as it is often referred to, has always intrigued me. My conviction is that, if a batsman can play well on a bad wicket, he should be able to play better on a good wicket. Some of the most valuable innings I have seen have been on bad wickets. What a delight it was to watch Herbert Sutcliffe and Wally Hammond batting on turf which gave the bowlers every advantage over any batsman not of the highest class. In such conditions Sutcliffe and Hammond showed their superiority over the majority of batsmen.

In my case, I just *had* to develop a technique to combat the rough, unprepared wickets. That was the essence of my early play. Each ball had to be watched closely. None could be trusted. I am sure that basic training did me good because, when I encountered similar conditions later in life, I overcame them reasonably well.

Until I broke my left arm in 1941, I always held the bat in a manner I believe to be the best. The v's formed by the index finger and thumb of both hands pointed down the handle in line with the back of the splice. With this grip, my left arm was employed to maximum advantage, and the 'wicked right' r bottom arm, the downfall of so many players, only when I wanted to add punch to the stroke.

After my arm was fractured, I had to move my left hand farther round the handle of the bat, so that the back of the hand faced cover-point. I never played so well again, certainly not as well as in 1939 which I thought was my best year as a batsman.

Many will not agree with this but, surely, the player knows best about himself. In 1939 I could play every stroke in the book as and when I wished. After my disablement I could not play certain shots the way I would have liked. It is not generally known that at the time I fractured my left fore-arm, the base of the ulna was dislocated and pushed down about an inch towards my little finger. There was a chance that I would be left with a stiff left wrist.

The surgeon fully understood the desperate position I would be in if I had to play with a locked left wrist. Accordingly an operation was performed to help the wrist's mobility and it succeeded in saving it from locking. But never again was I to know full movement of my left wrist.

When I began to play again I soon realized that some strokes, particularly the pull and the hook which I had played freely before the war, would not be possible again. On the quicker wickets of Australia they were bound to let me down. At best they are risky shots because the bat must be taken back into position quickly, a movement to which the left arm contributes substantially.

After the accident I found that the restricted movement of my wrist and fore-arm delayed the lifting of the bat just enough to make the shot hurried and uncontrolled. This often produced a half-hit to mid-wicket. One of the most important requirements when playing the pull stroke is, I think, a slight pause at the top of the back swing such as Don Bradman had. I found now that I had no time for that pause.

I tried a bat weighing only two pounds four ounces as against the two pounds six ounces I had used previously. I tried a Harrow size bat. But I found nothing that satisfactorily overcame the slowness of my upswing or helped me at the beginning of the back lift when the left hand plays its most vital part.

There was no alternative. I had to cut out the shot altogether.

In those long, dreary months, after my injury, when my left arm was encased in plaster from knuckle to shoulder, often looked at it and wondered just what the future held for me.

Cricket was my life. Would I ever be able to play properly again? My specialist, Mr. Broomhead, had done so much for me, yet I wondered whether even *he* realized then just how important that left arm was to me.

If only my right arm had been broken instead of the left. My destiny was wrapped up in that arm. The right arm is less important to a right-handed batsman like myself. To a right-hander, batting is essentially a left-handed game—and vice-versa.

Only in 1936, 1937 and 1939 was I completely free from some form of physical ache or injury. In the early part of the M.C.C. tour in South Africa in 1938–39, the first signs of my back trouble appeared. When I stooped quickly to stop a hard cover-drive, I felt a sharp pain in my lower right side. I was told that the trouble was a slight attack of lumbago, and it cleared up in a few days.

Almost twelve months later, while at home waiting for Army call up, I again stooped suddenly—and this time I could not stand up straight. I spent nearly a fortnight in bed until the pain eased.

I joined the Army in January 1940, and had little or no back worry until the spring of 1941, when an almost-permanent ache developed in the small of my back. This persisted to the time I reported at York for the Commando training during part of which I broke my arm.

While in hospital, I mentioned my back to the specialist and had massage, as well as heat treatment. Both helped, but the pain persisted whenever I stooped, or walked long distances, so manipulative surgery was decided upon. This eased my back, but did not completely relieve the ache and I have rarely been without pain during the last ten years.

The day after M.C.C.'s arrival in Tasmania, during the 1946–47 tour, I was again out of action. A severe pain affected the lower group of muscles in the small of my back, I could

feel it also in my left side, and where the pain was most acute
I found noticeable swelling.

Repeated attacks in the back struck me at intervals between
1947 and 1950 and the M.C.C., becoming concerned about my
fitness for the 1950–51 Australian tour, sent me to a well-known
London specialist, who diagnosed disc trouble.

He was far from certain I would be able to maintain the
required standard of fitness for such an exacting tour. Yet he
knew how much I wanted to be in the side for Australia and
I believe this, plus his own keenness for the game, influenced
him to pass me as fit to go.

He did, however, give me valuable information on how to
cope with disc trouble, and supplied me with yards of elastic
bandage, some of which was wrapped round me before I left
the consulting-room.

That elastic bandage played a big part in my success that
tour. I never went on to the field without it, and I did not suffer
one severe attack of lumbago. Since then, I have constantly
worn several yards of elastic bandage and a belt to support the
muscles in the small of the back.

Mid-way through the 1951 season I felt, for the first time,
a slight pain in my calf muscles. It gave me little immediate
concern and I did not associate it with my back. That winter,
however, I seriously considered retiring from first-class cricket.
My arm continued to be troublesome, especially when the
weather was severe, and the pains in both back and leg were
disturbing to say the least.

By the spring of 1952, however, I felt reasonably fit.
Early in the cricket season I was appointed captain of England
against India at Leeds, a distinction which gave me a new
lease of life and changed my views about retirement.

I realized that success as captain against India could
result in the honour being extended to me for the Australian
tour of England in 1953. The thought of being allowed to
organize an England team against Australia gave me the
greatest uplift I ever experienced. My sole dread was the state
of my back and its ability to sustain me.

Generally, in the summers of 1952 and 1953, I spent
Sundays in bed, unless a meeting of the England Selection
Committee took me to London. With the help of these rests

I managed to keep reasonably free from severe pain. Constan
treatment kept me going through the tour of West Indies and
in the following winters I am sure that, without the help o
the masseur, Harold Dalton, I would not have enjoyed the
fitness I did in Australia in 1954–55.

But severe recurrence of back trouble after my return to
England compelled me to withdraw from the captaincy for
the Test series with South Africa in 1955, and I was able to play
only a limited amount of county cricket. By the end of the
season, after further treatment, I was ordered to wear a plaster
jacket and in that I remained encased until a few days before
Christmas. I kept on hoping I would be fit enough by the spring
to play against the Australians. But, although my health made
substantial improvement, I knew in my heart of hearts that to
be perfectly fair to the public, my fellow-players and myself,
there was only one thing I could do. And, in the middle of
January, with great reluctance I announced my retirement.
Of that, more anon.

Yorkshire player, Oval, 1952

First time as England's captain *v.* India, Manchester, 1952

Captain of Yorkshire

First Test *v.* Australia, 1953

CHAPTER XI

THE BURDEN OF CAPTAINCY

I WAS a lucky man to play any post-war first-class cricket, after I fractured my left arm.

In 1944, the hopes I had entertained of making a cricket tour of Australia were diminishing. After a third operation on my arm a Yorkshire journalist came to see me in hospital and asked point-blank: "Do you think you will ever play first-class cricket again?" Although I was feeling extremely low-spirited I said I was determined to play again. Not only was I set upon doing so, but I had great confidence in Mr. R. Broomhead, the orthopædic surgeon in whose hands lay my future.

Largely through Mr. Broomhead's efforts I regained fitness and, by playing League or minor cricket once a week, I was able slowly to regain the standard necessary to resume my place in the Yorkshire and, eventually the England, Eleven.

The struggle to get back imposed a physical as well as a mental strain. I often said to myself: 'I'd give anything to be like so-and-so with a strong left arm.' Vain wishes, I knew, but frequently on arrival home after cricket I confided to my wife, Dorothy: "This arm is giving me hell." The pain always has been worse in cold or damp weather. Only in warmer climates than that of England have I been able to enjoy comparative freedom from pain.

*   *   *

Any burden that I felt about the captaincy of England since 1952, however, was increased by so many people suggesting *it was* a burden.

If I require advice about anything I make a point of going to the person best qualified to give it; but, as captain of England, I found myself the target for advice and instruction from many people who had never played in a Test, still less had the honour of captaining England. Doubtless all such advice was offered with best intentions, but usually it was not worth the paper on which it was written or the time spent over saying it. That is one certain opinion I would like to pass on to all future captains.

During a hold-up for rain in one of the 1953 Tests one famous journalist left the Press Box specially to come to the dressing-room to tell me which roller to use on the wicket! He must have overlooked that, as the umpires bore the responsibility of getting the turf ready as quickly as possible for the resumption, the rolling was their affair not mine.

Another time, at the end of a Test match at Lord's, the wife of a celebrated cricket personality asked me why I did not claim the extra half-hour. I imagined this was the outcome of some discussion she had overheard in which her husband had taken part. The rules of course do not allow for an extra half-hour in Test cricket but I pretended not to have heard. To all future England captains I say most emphatically: "Take notice only of those who have been 'under fire'."

Nor can success on the cricket field be achieved by off-the-field committees. When a man goes out to bat, he leaves his coach behind in the dressing-room!

*   *   *

In 1926, when I was barely ten, a cricket book was published that had a profound influence on my future. It was written by an ex-Australian captain, M. A. Noble—by a coincidence just a year after Lord Hawke made his observations on the possibility of England under professional leadership. 'Monty' Noble laid down a pattern which I followed long afterwards when destiny thrust me into the most coveted appointment in the game.

Noble's suggestions were such good sense, so much to the point, that I am repeating some of them at length here. The following extracts from *The Game's the Thing* are worth thinking about by captains in all games of cricket:

"No matter how genial he may be, a captain must command respect; he must at all times be dignified; indeed, his success is due in great measure to the fact that he is different from the majority of his fellow-cricketers. His personality impresses and the individuality of his methods are readily recognized by the members of his own team and, sooner or later by his opponents and by the general public, who are the final arbiters of his worth and fitness to command.

He must have initiative and sufficient mentality to plan comprehensive tactics, which will ensure harmonious working for strategical success. He must be alert and quick to sum up the weakness or strength in his opponents; he will know the exact moment for bold measures and recognize when caution must be the keynote. He must be quick in decision and determined in application, have an even temper and great self-control—calm in success and adversity.

One of the great failings of captains in general is that they work their best bowlers to a standstill. Who has not seen the star bowler in a side occupying the bowling crease from the beginning of play until the lunch adjournment with very little success, sometimes with none at all?

It is said in defence: 'Oh yes, but he always looked like getting a wicket'. 'Looking like it' isn't getting men out, and is no valid reason for putting him out of action for the rest of the day as an effective attacking force. Overworking a bowler is permissible only when wickets are falling rapidly.

All the followers of the game know the wonderful value of a captain who is adept in the art of placing a field for the different batsmen as they come in. Not only is he of great importance as a run-saving agent; his value is more comprehensive than that, for, when the batsman finds his main scoring strokes blocked, he is compelled to crawl into his shell and be content with an occasional loose one to score off, or—and this is just what the captain is after—he endeavours to make strokes which he is not sure of, or to make forcing strokes, which at all times are risky.

No captain, however clever he may be, can place a field for bad bowling. Inaccuracy in length and direction call out to the batsman to hit the ball anywhere he likes. . . .

If two batsmen require a differently placed field, and are constantly changing ends, the captain should insist upon each man taking his appointed place in the field for each batsman. A placed field for one is no earthly use for the other;

therefore, it is foolish to take the line of least resistance and omit to change the field out of consideration for the over-worked fieldsmen.

You cannot afford to be careless in big cricket; if you are, you will breed carelessness in the team and lose matches. Besides, good cricketers enjoy fielding and revel in plenty of work.

Many other instances could be cited to demonstrate the value of a knowledge of the idiosyncrasies of wickets to a captain but, of course, every individual situation has to be judged according to the circumstances surrounding it at the moment, so that no hard and fast rules can be laid down.

After all, strategy is a combination of instinct and experience, in the possession of which captains vary widely; yet no man can ever be a great captain without possessing both. Where a leader of a team is deficient in these qualities he sometimes tries to cover up his ineptitude by descending to what is generally known as 'pointing'. A team under such a captain will soon earn a bad reputation that may stick to it even after he has been superseded.

Excessive appealing is a habit very readily acquired by such a team and you can depend upon it that, when such a fault develops, the captain is primarily to blame. It is no use his figuratively hiding his head and hoping that the decision will be 'out' when he knows quite well that it should be nothing of the kind. By keeping quiet and allowing such appeals to be made, he is only condoning an evil and dishonest practice. It is the captain's job to discipline his men, to stamp out this unsportsmanlike habit and thus to aid in keeping the game clean.

If he lacks moral courage or shirks his responsibility in the hope of good coming for his team out of evil, he stands convinced by his team's behaviour, and it were better for the game that he had never played it.

A good reputation is very hard to win, and just as difficult to maintain, but it is very easy to lose. Besides, no man's character is impervious to bad influences. If he allows them to go unchecked, his own moral fibre must become weakened. The difference between reputation and character is this: Reputation is what other people believe you to be; character is what you know yourself to be.

A captain who makes no allowance for mistakes and is for ever grumbling discourages effort and honest endeavour.

If a batsman gets out in a foolish manner, or is trapped into doing something you have previously warned him against, do not, when he returns to the pavilion, rush at him and say: 'Why did you do this, or that?' He knows his mistake and feels it keenly, particularly if the game is going against your side. Leave him alone, let the lesson sink in, and next day have a quiet, sympathetic talk with him. It will do more good; you will earn his gratitude, and he will learn to respect you.

The captain who takes points on his opponents, only dishonours himself, and sooner or later will find that his actions will react to his own disadvantage.

If a player is selected and the captain does not think he should be in the team, or has a personal dislike for him, he must on no account allow his antipathy to influence his judgment. He must dissociate himself from any desire to see that he does not get a proper show; otherwise the team will be penalized. The main thing is to win the match; personal feelings have no place in cricket unless, perhaps, in very exceptional circumstances.

Never show preference for a friend. Always endeavour to act fairly and impartially to every unit of the team, classing them more as units than individuals. It is not easy to do this. A captain requires a strong mind and plenty of courage to forget all else in the team's best interests.

If you hold the balance well, both he with whom you are unfriendly as well as he with whom you are friendly and all the other members of the team will notice and appreciate your action. On the contrary, if you single a man out for any reprisal, however slight, they will notice that also and the confidence they have in you will be shaken.

There is nothing so humiliating to a captain as a public exhibition by one of his men who disagrees with an umpire's decision. How much more is it so to his team, to a State, or to a country, when a captain is guilty of a similar offence?''

*   *   *

So much for M. A. Noble. I accepted him, an Australian, as my guide in the matter of captaincy and I accepted an Englishman, Jack Hobbs, as my ideal as an opening batsman, even though I saw Hobbs play only once. That was at Bradford, where he made a late cut for four off Bill Bowes which I have never forgotten.

The first time I went to London to play at the Oval I deliberately sought out the great man. I did so because I felt he possessed unrivalled knowledge as an opening batsman. Before I met him I rehearsed all the things I wanted to talk about and, as an introduction, I took along the bat I had used when making my first century in first-class cricket only two weeks earlier.

Jack Hobbs autographed the bat for me in the dressing-room but, from that moment, I was almost completely tongue-tied. How foolish I felt! Here was this golden opportunity for which I had waited so patiently for years—and all I could say was a humble "Thank you very much for signing my bat!"

That first meeting with Jack Hobbs, however, helped me more than I realized at the time. Long afterwards, when I had become established as England's number one batsman, that memory enabled me better to understand young and aspiring cricketers and, in particular, to try and help them to overcome their shyness.

My recollection of Jack Hobbs from our first meeting at the historic Oval is of a quiet, friendly and unaffected man. To all in the dressing-room, players and groundsman alike, his attitude was the same—in many respects very similar to that of Wilfrid Rhodes, who was prepared to talk about cricket on the odd occasion but could never easily be drawn. Patsy Hendren once remarked: "Wilfrid Rhodes doesn't say very much but when he does—listen." I accepted Patsy's advice.

*   *   *

My first game as an England player in 1937 and my first Test as England's captain fifteen years later had one thing in common—my failure as a batsman.

Against New Zealand at Lord's in 1937 I made nought and

one; against India in 1952, I scored only ten in each innings, failures, which I am sure, were due to tension.

Believe it or not, when I was told I had been selected to appear for my country in a Test I experienced such a thrill that I promptly lost my appetite!

My last county game before the Test with New Zealand in 1937 was at Hull, after which I travelled to London to join the rest of the England team. On the morning of the match I could hardly eat. This feeling of tension persisted as I set off with my cricket bag for Lord's. The moment I left the taxi outside the 'W. G. Grace Gates' I was gripped by an awful feeling of fright. I wanted to run away. I wondered: 'Am I doing right in going in here?'

I felt so insignificant by comparison with the bowler-hatted men, carrying rolled umbrellas and escorting expensively dressed women, who walked past me and, in many cases, were recognized by the gate-keeper. For me, no recognition from the gatekeeper, only a raised eyebrow that seemed to say: "Who's this odd-looking character?" If the gatekeeper had only known how nervous I was he might have given me a word or two of cheer!

Previously at Lord's I had used the dressing-room normally set outside for county players. When I made my way there this time I was told that, as this was a Test match, I was to use the amateurs' dressing-room upstairs.

That meant everything was different, down to the attendant. I soon began to feel I was in the wrong house altogether— until I was handed a pile of 'good luck' telegrams. That made me much happier but it didn't kill the tension which nagged at me all through my first Test at Lord's.

After my inglorious duck in my first Test innings I went alone to a cinema, to sit quietly in the dark to reflect upon my misery. I settled myself comfortably. Fifteen minutes later, a newsreel shot of the Test match was shown. I got up and walked out.

*   *   *

My first Test as captain of England in 1952 should have been perfect. Had I been asked to nominate a ground I could hardly have done other than say: 'Headingley, Leeds', as familiar to me as my back garden. Yet the fact that there were so many people who knew me and wanted to talk to me had the opposite effect to what might have been imagined.

To a player, like myself, schooled in Yorkshire cricket, making a debut as England's captain at Headingley was a handicap, not an advantage. Frankly, I was scared of doing the wrong thing and the strain affected me. All the back-slapping, the good wishes, the entreaties of: "Don't forget to make a century for us, Len," and the rest only created in me a mighty caution.

Remarks like: "I've coom forty mile to see thee bat. Now, think on, get some runs," coming from my own Yorkshire folk, put pressure on me, making the individual appear to be more important than the team and the result of the match.

I could not help thinking: 'What if I get a shooter first ball or the other batsman runs me out? What if a-hundred-and-one other things happen? All these people are going to feel that I have let them down.'

After the Headingly Test my batting improved considerably. I scored 150 in the first innings of the next Test at Lord's, 104 at Manchester and 86 at the Oval.

How can a highly enthusiastic crowd, such as were at Headingley, know the problems besetting a new captain or understand that the captain's main function is to produce that extra something from the *other* members of the team, and not to go in for record-breaking performances himself?

This wish to get the best from the team is not easy to accomplish in England because the captain meets the players collectively for the first time only a few hours before the beginning of the match. On tour, the position is different, since the skipper practically lives with his team all the time.

As England's captain, I have, during Tests, made a mental note as various points cropped up with the intention of discussing them later with the individual players.

Even when all the players can be assembled, however, I do not favour a detailed discussion at which the whole team collects. I have always preferred the personal approach to individual players, and I have concentrated my efforts on the youngsters.

No doubt some people would like the England captain to

follow the tactical example of the football manager and allot his team their tasks for the following day, but I cannot agree with such an idea. Experience taught me that any off-the-field plan can go astray in a few minutes on the field. My view is that too much pre-match planning makes a team into a collection of blueprints lacking flexibility as individuals.

The captain's main purpose must be to encourage and improve each player to use his intelligence for the general betterment of the team.

The skipper must also try to set the type of field he knows a bowler ought to have, yet make it appear as if the bowler himself has got what he wanted.

I have often told a bowler I would soon be moving a fielder a yard or so without consulting him further, and have told him not to worry or wonder why. I have stressed to the bowler: "I'm working as hard as you to get a wicket." In other words, I have been trying to 'kid' him that he is getting what he wants rather than what I want for him. After all, bowlers are temperamental, especially when they 'feel' the tension of the crowd, and they must be handled very carefully.

I have made a point always to ask a bowler what sort of field he wanted. When he has asked for something I considered to be wrong or a waste of resources, usually I have managed, with his tacit co-operation, to get what I felt he *ought* to have.

Some captains are known to place the field for a bowler, irrespective of his wishes or without consulting him; but, by pursuing this policy, they only succeed in decreasing the bowler's efficiency. A bowler's wishes must always be considered most carefully.

*   *   *

Talking of tactics reminds me of the times I have left the pavilion fully determined how I should bat—only to change my ideas radically as soon as I reached the middle.

I remember how Ernie Toshack annoyed the England batsmen by persistently bowling at and just outside the leg stump in Australia in 1946–47. I decided, therefore, to take guard six inches outside the leg stump so that—as I told the other players in the dressing-room—I could hit Toshack to the off. My plan failed when Toshack countered by pitching the ball six inches wider on the leg-side!

Again, in the second innings of the Second Test at Lord's in 1948, I made up my mind before going in to bat to attack Lindwall, Miller, and Johnston. All I managed to do was to play myself out of the next Test. In each case the lesson was not to make up my mind beforehand.

Experience in a captain is not as important as many seem to imagine. More important is knowledge of the game and the ability to assess the qualities of your own players as well as those of the opposition.

Leadership is hardest when the task is to get the other side out in conditions favouring batsmen. Then it is vital that a captain should be able to detect when a bowler is having little effect on the batsmen. This, in itself, could help to explain certain bowling changes which apparently mystify onlookers not seeped in cricket knowledge and experience.

Wickets also fall through the fielding side being able to bring off a surprise. In Test cricket this is a most difficult accomplishment but the captain must constantly be working towards this end—to create confusion in the mind of the batsmen.

*   *   *

Having mentioned the comparative unimportance of experience in captaincy I should emphasize that I am speaking only of captaincy in saying that. Whenever a young cricketer 'hits' the newspaper headlines and reads that he is being considered for representative honours, I begin to wonder: 'How much criticism has the lad had to face?' If he has withstood some 'fire', I believe he is better equipped to stand up to the criticism which is the inevitable part of Test cricket.

The further north in England, the more severe becomes the criticism. In the North critics can either 'make you' or 'break you'. On the other hand, I believe that the South or West Country cricketer, so often reared on praise, is shocked when he is adversely criticized. Accordingly, he grows resentful and becomes dispirited, instead of shrugging his shoulders and saying: "It was bound to come some time."

Half the battle in Test cricket is in becoming acclimatized to its stresses and the ability to take the good with the bad.

A tendency today is for players to want to talk less and less about the game. The reason is that those in the top flight are reacting from a surfeit of cricket compared with pre-war days. That, coupled with an increased amount of newspaper criticism, has added to the strain of Test cricket. Many cricketers, as a result, want nothing more than to relax mentally, as well as physically, when they are not on the field.

It is difficult enough during a Test to get away completely from the game. Press, radio and TV critics and almost everyone else talk about the play for hours on end, when the players wish for nothing more than to forget about it until next morning.

Another trouble nowadays is the constant talk of 'technique'. I think we are beginning to lose sight, if we have not already done so, of the fact that cricket was intended to be a simple, uncomplicated, summer party. On village greens up and down the country it still is. But villagers aren't plagued by theorists!

If Denis Compton had been a different man, the technicians easily might have ruined his style of play—and what a tragedy that would have been for England cricket! I say that when a player like Denis reaches international standards he should, from the coaching viewpoint, be stroke-proof.

There are, of course, one or two fundamentals which must be observed. The eye, for example, must be along the line of the ball.

To assist this I would always advocate an upright stance—no crouch—and for most purposes a leg-stump guard. This prevents the head from moving outside the line and from beyond the off-stump, committing the batsman to on-side play.

I would stamp on any tendency to move laterally across the stumps rather than up and down the pitch; and I would emphasize the importance of keeping the 'extremities', head, hands and feet, so placed that a vertical line drawn up from the ground would pass through them. Otherwise I would allow any young batsman to develop the strokes which come most easily to him.

*   *   *

In many ways I have found the captaincy of England a harder task at home than overseas. That is because of the changeable English climate. Here many matches begin on a rain-affected wicket and frequently a captain, winning the toss, is faced with a difficult decision. In county games, the chances are he would put the other side in.

Even so I was rarely confronted with a problem about choice of innings during my first two seasons as England's captain. I lost the toss seven times out of nine! The only toss I won against Lindsay Hassett in 1953 was that I have mentioned—the 'dummy' throw at the Oval. As Lindsay called 'heads' on that occasion I thought that to be a sufficiently good omen and ever after I called 'tails'. Eventually my luck broke even. I was twice right in the West Indies in 1953–54 and three times in Australia in 1954–55.

Some years ago when I was sitting with George Hirst in a tram-car on the way from Headingley to the City centre in Leeds he advised me against becoming superstitious about the game but it has not been easy. For instance, I have been presented with scores of coins of different denominations, each accompanied by a letter assuring me that if I used it I could not fail to win the toss for England.

Of those many varied coins—a five-shilling piece, half-crowns, even a Chinese sovereign—the one I always kept was given to me by Mr. Fisher, one of my best supporters during my early days with the local club in my native Pudsey St. Lawrence. Mr. Fisher's reward to me for scoring fifty in an important match was a five-shilling piece. When he gave it to me he commented: "Don't part with it until you are down to your last five shillings." That is exactly what happened.

In January 1940 I was in the Army and stationed at Aldershot. I kept my five-shilling piece in a top pocket of my battle-dress tunic. Later I was moved to Lincoln where, going out one night for a game of snooker, I found I had no money, other than the said five-shilling piece.

To pay my share, I asked my opponent to change the coin on the understanding that he would return it next day. Back at camp that night, I was detailed to report to York for a Commando course. Within twenty-four hours I was on my way—without my large silver coin. Five days later, in training, came the mishap to my arm which caused me pain and anxiety for a long time. The five-shilling piece was forgotten.

Ten years later, in 1952, an hour before the start of the Second Test against India at Lord's, I received a letter with a Lincoln postmark. Inside I found my five-shilling piece. I suppose it should have brought me luck when I spun it for Vizay Hazare to call. It didn't do so then but I continued using it and my luck changed in the last two tosses of that series.

*   *   *

Captaincy of England through four series of Tests was a wonderful experience, and I have mentioned elsewhere my gratitude to M.C.C. for their magnificent support.

I must, however, single out two distinguished players of the past who have also been very kind to me, Sir Pelham Warner and Sir William Worsley. I have had little contact with Sir Pelham Warner during the past three years but I shall always treasure his friendship. When I made my nervous Test debut in 1937, he encouraged me enormously and never ceased trying to be helpful.

Sir William Worsley, of Hovingham Hall, near York, an ex-captain of Yorkshire, has also taken the keenest interest in my career. His frequent letters when I was on tour meant a great deal to me.

An England captain must suffer a wealth of criticism, not all of it deserved or kind. But when he has expressions of friendship like these behind him, he is fortified to withstand the less pleasant side of the job.

CHAPTER XII

FORM AND CAPTAINCY

OFTEN during the last three years I have heard it said that the cares of captaincy were having a bad effect on my batting. Many people wrote to me in this strain and I suppose there is something in their argument. The captaincy of any cricket team, whether it be in a club, county or Test match, does entail a responsibility which the other members of the team are spared.

I think I found the dual burden most arduous in 1952, my first year of captaincy. My appointment received a great deal of publicity and from the first it was asked whether my batting would stand the strain. Somehow this worried me more than the fact that I was a professional occupying a position previously held by amateurs. So many of the great amateur captains of the past went out of their way to be kind and helpful to me that my anxieties on that score were soon dispelled.

Amongst them were D. R. Jardine, the hero of my boyhood; A. P. F. Chapman, whose personality and charm will be remembered so well by all who came in close contact with him; and Arthur Gilligan, with whom I have travelled on three tours to Australia and whose advice I found invaluable on my last tour. He has in his quiet way done much for cricket in general since his retirement.

Many kind words of encouragement came from George Mann, with whom I toured South Africa in 1948–49. They were of immense help and were particularly prized since they came from a man greatly respected by all who have been fortunate enough to play under and with him.

I have already told of my feelings before and during my First Test as captain at Headingley when I was weighed down by my desire to make runs on my home ground and before my fellow-Yorkshiremen. But that feeling soon passed and in the next Test at Lord's I made my first century as captain.

In the subsequent series I think my record shows that I

carried the burden fairly easily—in the West Indies I was able to average ninety-six in the Tests. Some might say that the cumulative effect did not show until the Australian tour but I think only part of my moderate batting then can be attributed to the worries of captaincy.

At that time I was not often free from some sort of ache in the lower regions of my back. Keith Miller remarked to me on one occasion while I was batting that I did not appear to be seeing the ball quite as early as I used to. His remarks did not help me to see the ball any earlier but, nevertheless, there was probably something in what he said.

It was, however, in Australia in 1954-55 that I had perhaps my hardest task as captain. I had always found that the Selection Committee meetings where intricate and important decisions had to be made were the most testing part of the captaincy. In England it was not so bad, for there were with me older men than myself who shared the responsibility. In Australia the main responsibility was mine.

On many tours the Test team more or less selects itself. Not, however, on this one—and, after Brisbane, I had to take the fairly hard decision of leaving out the great Alec Bedser, my comrade at arms for so many years. I have already told of my weeks of worry both before and after the decision was taken.

I have been looking through my batting figures as captain of England and I think perhaps they give the answer to the question. The responsibility of captaincy did affect my batting, but not immediately nor consistently.

CHAPTER XIII

FOUR-DAY TESTS—HOURS OF PLAY —AND WHEN TO PLAY

IF the choice was left to me I would limit all Test matches in England to four days, always to start on a Friday.

Five-day Tests were introduced in the hope of bringing about more definite decisions. The argument was that, as two county programmes were already cut into in four-day games, an extra day would give more chance of an outright result without interfering further with domestic cricket. Beginning in 1950, however, all Test series in England have been arranged on a five-day basis.

In the main, the purpose appears to have been achieved. What may have been overlooked is that, although the extension gave each captain additional opportunity to win the match, it also increased his caution not to take any risk which might lead to defeat. The outcome has been a tendency towards the tempo of the game becoming slower. That is a bad thing and we must look for remedies.

My belief is that a restriction to four days would minimize the risks attached to each and every action in the match. As a result, teams would, I think, regain most of the attacking approach which characterized Test cricket some twenty years ago, especially if certain changes in the rules were made. Such changes as I suggest I will detail later.

Twenty years ago the scoring of 400 runs a day was not the sensation it would be in Test cricket today and, if four-day Tests were the rule, I cannot think we should find a preponderance of draws. We must not overlook that, in the last series of four-day Tests, against South Africa in 1947, three games finished with a definite result.

From an England point of view, a big advantage of a return to four-day Tests would be to give the leading players more rest before each match.

How well I remember Alec Bedser turning up at Trent

The team which won the Ashes, Oval, 1953

Balcony jubilations after England's win

Body balance is essential

At home in Pudsey with Dorothy, Richard and John

This one should knock out that middle stump . . .

. . . but not if you hold the bat this way

Bridge the day before the First Test with the Australians in 1953. He had been in the field at the Oval throughout the previous day and, in the Northamptonshire second innings which began at tea on the second day and lasted until the end of the match, he had bowled thirty-seven overs. I was anxious to go into the nets for ten minutes or so batting practice against Alec, but he was so weary when he sank into the dressing-room chair that I just hadn't the heart to ask him. All he wanted to do was rest.

Before the start of the match, in fact, not more than five of the England team looked to me thoroughly fresh and 'rarin' to go'. The others sat around in the dressing-room, unmistakably thinking of the five days' hard work ahead. Had they come to the ground after a few days' rest, I am sure they would have been much more energetic. It has always amazed me that Alec bowled as well as he did then—this was the occasion of his fourteen wickets for 99. Even so, he was a very tired man the day before the game began and, had he not struck success early in the match, he might have flagged in his effort, without realizing he was doing so.

By contrast to England on the day before the Nottingham Test opened the Australians were as lively as ever, thoroughly eager to get on to the field and on with the job.

Australian cricketers have often said to me: "We don't know how your players manage to play cricket six days a week, season after season. We just couldn't stand it." Certainly, the Australians are never required to do so when visiting England. Usually seventeen players are brought on the tour, which gives each man a chance to rest between matches. England players, on the other hand, have their county commitments to fulfil, and the county programme today leaves little time for relaxation. And the professional cricketer, employed by his county club, cannot ask for time off to prepare for a Test match. Counties look upon their Test players as extra attractions to would-be spectators and they feel they cannot afford to be without their Test men for longer than is absolutely necessary. As it is, the counties often have to be without regular Test players for anything up to ten matches a season—more if the same players are required for Test Trials, Gentlemen v. Players and other representative games.

I

Finance plays such a vital part in the organization of Test cricket, however, that I fear my suggestion to play only four-day Tests is not likely to be adopted. My alternative, if five-day Tests are to continue, would be to reduce the number of playing hours.

A start could be made each day at twelve o'clock, instead of eleven-thirty, and stumps drawn at six o'clock, instead of six-thirty as at present, aggregating five hours daily, as in Australia. Twelve to six is, to my mind, ideal for cricket.

*   *   *

One other major alteration should, I believe, be made to the existing regulations for Test matches. I would like to see all matters relating to the state of the ground in Test cricket left to the discretion of the umpires, instead of to the rival captains.

Early in my career as captain of England I received striking evidence of the complications the present system can lead to, by the happenings at the Oval in 1952 in the last Test against India. After a thunderstorm at lunch on the second day, the ground dried well and I wanted to get on with the cricket again quickly, because I felt that the pitch was sufficiently dry for England to bowl on. To make certain I took Alec Bedser to the middle to see whether he could get a proper foothold for his run-up to the crease. Alec said he felt certain he would be able to bowl normally.

When I returned to the dressing-room I told the other England players that the pitch was all right but that they had to be careful about the outfield, which was greasy. I was surprised when the India captain, Vijay Hazare, held up England's preparations to field by saying that he did not want to play because in his view the wicket was not fit for batting.

I find difficulty in believing that a wicket considered fit for bowling is unfit for batting. Doubtless Hazare's intention was to secure a further delay. In that he succeeded and the resumption was delayed for about an hour longer than I considered justified.

Another instance of what I thought to be unnecessary delay occurred at Nottingham in the First Test in 1953 against

Australia. After thrilling cricket of low scores, England were left more than two days in which to score 229 to win. When we began batting on the Saturday, the pitch had lost some of its earlier difficulties and, by the close, we were 42 for one, well on the way to victory, or so we thought.

Alas for our hopes! Rain fell heavily all through Monday and again during Monday night. On Tuesday, the last day, Lindsay Hassett showed no desire to resume quickly. On the other hand, I was anxious to begin again as soon as possible. Lindsay and I disagreed over the fitness of the pitch and left a decision to the umpires.

Lindsay's object, no doubt, was first to save Australia from the defeat that all the England team, at least, felt was certain to come. Secondly he must have wanted to limit the amount of time available for England to get the remaining 187 runs, and thus put us in a position in which, in order to win, we would have to go for the runs faster than we could with reasonable safety. In such circumstances, he could well have reckoned that we might take undue risks, lose wickets in our scramble and become undecided whether to race for runs. This could have opened the door to Australia to snatch a dramatic win.

Normally, I believe, the umpires would have said: "Play on" earlier than they did but, because of the disagreement between the captains, they had to be careful not to give the slightest advantage to either side. I think that, as a result, they hesitated that little extra. In the end, England were left with only another two hours' batting—play started on the last day at 4.30 p.m.—to make the runs. The task was beyond us, against defensive bowling on a slow wicket.

In my opinion the almost inevitable delay of anything up to three-quarters of an hour which follows disagreement between the two captains on the fitness of the pitch is helpful only to the skipper who wants to wait. After disagreement between the captains, the umpires would be unusual if they did not lean towards caution.

Lindsay Hassett and I disagreed again on the question of ground-fitness in the 1953 series of Tests. This was on the last day at Manchester where, although the issue was not as important as at Nottingham—a draw seemed inevitable—I wanted to get on with the game after rain sooner than did Lindsay. Again the disagreement between the captains left the decision to the umpires, and again I think they naturally hesitated longer than the state of the pitch warranted. This allowed more respite for the team not wishing to resume quickly.

I feel that in first-class cricket it is important for all captains to think more than some do about the crowd which has paid to watch. I believe that after an interruption the captains should try to get on with the game as soon as possible.

The crowd's attitude inevitably is: 'We've paid our money, your duty is to get on with the game', and I have much sympathy for such spectators. When people pay to watch any public entertainment they are entitled to the utmost consideration, and cricket authorities—and cricketers—must realize they are putting on a public performance in which not a moment should be lost.

Spectators at cricket have a good instinct for knowing which captain is responsible for continued delay and their reaction may result in a certain amount of 'crowd pressure' on that unfortunate (or unwise) individual who is responsible for the hold-up.

*   *   *

The most surprising thing about the Manchester Test of 1953 was the Australian second innings collapse—after the long delay—when they lost eight wickets for 35 runs on a pitch taking spin. Their struggles surprised me, even though I had seen them in trouble before, but on pitches much worse than at Old Trafford.

The Australian failure gave the England team, the Selectors and the English cricket public a big boost in morale. The realization that the Australians, who had not been beaten in a Test series by England since 1932, could be defeated was most encouraging to the players.

It was remarkable to watch how the Australian batsmen, nurtured on the good, hard wickets of their own country, reacted. Their batting revealed limitations in defensive technique, the main fault being that they were not skilled at dead-bat play against the ball that 'stopped'—an essential requirement of batting on rain-affected pitches.

Not until a batsman can play well on all types of pitches can he be described as a 'great' player. At Manchester most of the Australians played defensively at the ball with their bats *in motion* when these should have been dead and held loosely in relaxed fingers. Moreover, they did not get near enough to the pitch of the ball or watch its progress closely enough after pitching. Consequently, they were unable to delay their strokes until the last split-second, which is the essence of batting on a bad wicket.

The Australian batting at Manchester emphasized that, collectively, they were immature in the finer arts of defence under difficulties, as we understand the meaning of the expression. But never forget that what the Australians lack in technical skill they make up for with tremendous enthusiasm and determination to win.

CHAPTER XIV

THE NEW L.B.W. LAW

My retirement from first-class cricket has made it easier to offer my views on a point of cricket law which, in my opinion, has had more effect on modern batting than any other. I refer to the change in the l.b.w. law in 1935. Although I had little first-class cricket experience of the old law, I am certain that conditions are much more difficult for batsmen now than before the law was altered.

The first-class batsman of today has to think and work desperately hard for any success that comes to him. Great innings on rain-affected pitches have, through the bowler's exploitation of the new l.b.w. law, become almost non-existent. In recent years I have been satisfied if I have made thirty or forty runs on a wicket favouring bowlers. Before the change in the l.b.w. law big scores on bad wickets were by no means uncommon.

Older people often ask whether any of the present generation is capable of batting as well as Hobbs and Sutcliffe under similar conditions. With all respect to their skill, let it not be forgotten that Hobbs and Sutcliffe made many runs on rain-affected turf *before* the alteration in the l.b.w. law. I maintain that, if the old rule had remained, the best players of today would prove just as skilful at overcoming the difficulties of a tricky pitch as were some of the old masters.

Similarly, I feel that much of the blame for the slow rate of scoring in modern first-class cricket can be laid at the door of the revised l.b.w. law.

Until 1935, a batsman could be out leg-before only if the ball pitched between wicket and wicket. Some batsmen took advantage of this to 'pad off', or allow to pass, a great number of balls pitched outside the off-stump. The ruling authorities sought to stamp out such methods of being able to avoid playing at the ball.

Accordingly, the law was altered so that a bowler could

also get an l.b.w. decision with a ball pitched outside the off-stump which would, in the umpire's opinion, have hit the wicket had it not struck the batsman's body. The only stipulation was that the part of the body except the hands struck by the ball should be between wicket and wicket at the moment of impact.

The increased chance of getting such decisions gave greater incentive to off-spin and in-swing bowlers, but the l.b.w. law, as it now stands, has also made batsmen *think* much harder; and the harder they are required to *think* about their play, the fewer risks they are inclined to take. That, in turn, brings about a slower rate of scoring.

A certain period of time must elapse before the effect of any major change in cricket becomes apparent and I estimate that four or five years went by before the present l.b.w. law was thoroughly absorbed. The main reason for this was that bowlers who had perfected their arts before the change in the law did not speedily bridge the gap; for a time they continued to follow orthodox lines, rather like the batsman who, after the age of eighteen or so, begins to put into practice and to profit by what he has learned previously.

I played only one season in first-class cricket under the old l.b.w. law—that of 1934. Up to that time all the books of instruction emphasized the importance of playing back to the spinning ball on a turning wicket. Came the change in law, and even the batting masters found themselves given out leg-before far more frequently than hitherto.

The change, indeed, was considerable for those like Herbert Sutcliffe, whose batting had been based on back-leg theories that applied during the lifetime of the old l.b.w. law.

Under the old law a batsman could stand with his weight on the back leg and be in position for the hook stroke against fast bowlers—Herbert Sutcliffe was always 'half-way there' for the hook before the ball was bowled.

Herbert, who did not drive often, always stood with his weight on his front foot. Thus he was caught out of position by the new law. Still standing in the same way, he was not always able to counter the ball moving into him off the seam or breaking in late from the off. Time and again he was leg-before playing back to balls which previously would not have won the umpire's decision because they did not pitch in line between wicket and wicket.

The best stance under the new law has been found to be evenly balanced so that you can go forward or back with equal facility but, in the 1936 season, Herbert Sutcliffe was leg-before ten times—eight of them under the new law. His average dropped from fifty to thirty and he had his worst season in county cricket. The truth is that players of his generation simply could not be expected to change, at a late stage in their careers, the style of batting which had served them so well for so long.

In the days of the old law if a new bowler went into the nets at Headingley and bowled only in-swingers, the county talent scouts were not greatly interested in him. They wanted bowlers who were able to make the ball move the other way —the out-swinger. I have many times heard one of those responsible for engaging new professionals for Yorkshire ask George Hirst: "Have you discovered any bowlers, George?" and the answer was always the same. "Yes, but they are all in-swingers."

Under the old rule also a batsman could sweep at will against a round-the-wicket left-arm bowler. If he missed his stroke the verdict invariably was 'Not out'. Umpires took the view that, because of the ball's trajectory, if it pitched between wicket and wicket, as the law required, it would almost certainly miss the stumps and go down the leg-side, except on a pitch from which the ball would turn back sharply.

Thus under the old law, the efficient batsman normally could sweep with impunity on a good pitch and the left-arm bowlers could not afford to pack the off-side field. They were compelled to split their field forces and, in so doing, they allowed more gaps for scoring.

Nowadays, the sweep is very risky. On good pitches when the ball will not turn much left-arm slow bowlers pack the off-side with fieldsmen and aim to pitch just outside the off-stump. As long as the batsman is content to play the ball at a packed field, and wait for occasional runs, the danger is small, but when he tries to sweep, he takes far greater risks. If the ball is pitched a shade outside the off-stump and he misses his stroke, he will be leg-before, should the umpire think the ball would have carried on and hit the wicket. Previously, the same ball, having pitched outside the 'line', did not qualify for an l.b.w. decision.

Closely linked with the increase of in-swing and off-spin bowlers has been a big rise, particularly since the war, in the number of leg-side fielders. This applies especially to the use of two backward short legs. When facing a new ball attack, a batsman rarely does not find those two fieldsmen virtually at his elbow. The batsman who uses a high back-lift is an easy victim for either of them, especially against a new bowler of the Alec Bedser class.

The high back-lift is a style long favoured by the Public Schools and Universities. I am sure that the classic batsmen of previous generations would have had to curtail it to be successful in modern cricket. A high back-lift means that the bat must come a long way down, and, once down, move on in an upward arc. The ball thus hits a moving bat and may carry some distance afterwards.

With the short back-lift the bat does not make such a full swing and much less chance exists of the ball going any appreciable distance. Sir Donald Bradman, Walter Hammond and Herbert Sutcliffe, all great batsmen of the past twenty-five years, only lifted the bat high when they intended hitting the ball hard. There is little point in doing so otherwise.

Ironically, by the mischance of bad umpiring, the present l.b.w. law often operated in school and club cricket long before it made its official appearance in first-class cricket. Today, when there are so many off-spin and in-swing bowlers, the coaching of young batsmen is harder than it was years ago.

If a boy is taught to play forward to the off-spinner, he is in danger of giving a catch 'round the corner' to one of the short-leg fieldsmen. That is, unless he is an expert at dead-bat play; few schoolboys are. If, however, he is encouraged to play back to the same type of ball, he is immediately vulnerable under the present l.b.w. law.

As both in-swing and off-spin bowling can be delivered so accurately they have imposed shackles on the batsman both directly and indirectly. Directly, for some of the reasons I have given and indirectly because they have emphasized the comparative expensiveness of the leg-break bowler.

Leg-breaks are so much harder to bowl accurately than off-breaks that leg-break bowlers cannot be relied upon to 'close up' the game. Whereas the off-spinner can be expected to keep the batsman fairly quiet, the leg-spinner is bound to give him occasional freedom from his bonds.

Sir Donald Bradman suggested that the leg-break bowler could be helped by extending the scope of the present l.b.w. law to include balls which pitch outside the *leg*-stump. This would, I feel, be going too far. The batsman must put his legs somewhere and, in any case, the good-length ball going away from the bat is already so much harder to play than the ball coming into the body.

No, my suggestion is this—to return to the old l.b.w. rule and to extend, by the width of another stump, the area covered by the three stumps, making the total width of the wicket twelve inches instead of nine.

I do not advocate doing this by adding a stump, but by making the present stumps proportionately thicker. They could be thickened by an inch in diameter so that the gap between them would not be increased—otherwise the ball might go through. There is no need to alter the present height of the stumps; they are high enough already.

The introduction of wider wickets, would, I am sure, do much to lead cricket back to its previous position in which attack was considered the best form of defence.

If wickets were widened and a return made to the old l.b.w. law, no longer would any advantage be offered to the bowler who consistently pitched off the target. Such a stimulating move would tend to bring the leg-spinner more into the game, increase the dividends for bowling straight, and generally 'attacking' the batsman and encourage batsmen to make strokes.

Certainly, the larger target would add to the attractiveness of bowling and help to remove the present-day stalemate where the main plan seems to be 'let the crowd get him out'.

I feel that, if the batsman shows little desire to hit the ball, the bowler should try to make him do so.

The bowler who bowls wide of the stumps and takes the view that his opponent will get fed up with the position before he himself does is not helping the game win public favour.

THE NEW L.B.W. LAW

Surely, if the bowler could be encouraged at the sight of a twelve-inch wide wicket, he would be risking an early exit from the game by continuing to bowl off the target.

For 108 years three stumps have been used in cricket. Between 1823 and 1931 they were twenty-seven inches high and eight inches wide. Then another inch was added both to height and width. I believe a better alternative would have been to have added more to the dimensions of the stumps. In my view the game would be helped if that was done now.

*   *   *

My view is that the time has come to make matters more difficult for those left-arm over-the-wicket bowlers, who bowl from the edge of the crease and down the leg-side—that is, to a right-hander—of the batsman. Bowling down the leg-side, or 'straight' from their angle of delivery, they can keep the ball so far away from the batsman that he cannot hope to reach it with any certainty of making a scoring stroke.

If these left-arm over-the-wicket bowlers were forced to bowl from a point nearer the stumps, they would have to bowl at an angle instead of 'straight', as they do at present, in order to pitch defensively outside the leg-stump. That is a much more difficult thing to do. Consequently they would be likely either to pitch more often within the batsman's reach or to pitch too far out and be called for a wide.

Thus my other hope is for a reduction in the width of the bowling crease. In 1902 the line each side of the stumps was extended by one foot to four foot. I would like to see a return to the former measurement.

By a return to the old l.b.w. law, wider wickets and a reduction of the bowling crease, I believe the game would become better for the players and more enjoyable for the spectators. At the same time, it would retain its essential character. Cricket would be played at a livelier pace, and I think everyone would be happier.

*   *   *

You may wonder how I, such an advocate of measures to speed the game, came to be accused of wasting time, as I was both when I led the England team in the West Indies in 1953–54 and in Australia in 1954–55.

In each instance, I claim misunderstanding on the part of an impatient crowd. In the West Indies, the spectators made so much noise that every time I wanted to say something to a bowler, as I frequently did, I had to walk over to him from my position at mid-off. Otherwise he could not hear me. Hence, delay—and even more noise!

In Australia in 1954–55, in the Fourth Test at Adelaide, which Australia had to win to retain a chance of regaining the Ashes, I was accused of 'playing slowly and holding up the game'. The suggestion was that my strategy for success was to get the batsmen 'down' by the deliberate use of slow tactics.

My attitude is that every ball bowled in a cricket match should be part of an overall plan. The longer the game lasts, the more important this factor becomes.

If a bowler is not sure of his requirements in field-placings, the captain must advise him as much as possible. I tried to help all my bowlers to get the best out of themselves. That accounted for my frequent conferences with them.

In any case, could anyone expect that in the heat of Australia, Frank Tyson and Brian Statham would *run* back to their starting places? Both naturally take some time to return to their bowling marks and both need a momentary respite before bowling the next ball. Surely fast bowlers are not expected to canter back? Ray Lindwall never did, nor to my knowledge, did any other fast bowler.

CHAPTER XV

CRICKETERS AND THE PRESS

JUST as some regular topers say that no such thing exists as a 'bad' brew—they insist the only difference is that some brews are better than others—so some people in the public eye declare that no such thing exists as bad publicity. They take the view that they would rather be mentioned adversely by the critics than not be mentioned at all.

I am not convinced of the soundness of that argument, but I believe that cricketers, like anyone else in the public eye, must be prepared to accept praise and criticism with equal grace, not allowing the one to cause a need for a larger county cap, or the other to represent anything more than a friendly rap on the knuckles, which, even if undeserved, never hurt anybody.

For any public figure to attack the Press is incautious, to say the least. Anyone who resorts to such an attack may gain satisfaction by having temporarily hit back at his critics, but in the end the critics will have the last say—and the last laugh. Their columns are open to them every day of the week and for years to come.

After twenty-five years of close association with the British Press, I know of no journalist who wittingly has done me harm as a cricketer. Many have done me a wealth of good and have given me considerable pleasure and entertainment by their writing.

For instance, I shall read Mr. R. C. Robertson-Glasgow and Mr. Neville Cardus as long as they are spared to regale us with their brilliant style of sports journalism. I hope that my two sons, John and Richard, will enlarge their knowledge and love of the game by following cricket through the eyes of these two great writers.

When I say this, don't think that I have always agreed with the opinions of all cricket writers. That is far from the case. But I do believe that the great majority are doing an honest job of work, and one which is far more difficult than is appreciated by the majority of those who speak disparagingly of 'The Press'. To satisfy an Editor, the public—and the players—all the time is nearly an impossible combination but, I repeat, I have no complaints. 'The Press' have done me proud.

As a youngster, I was always anxious to read every scrap of information about the famous players. This was particularly so when an M.C.C. side went abroad in the English winter. If I opened my newspaper and failed to find anything about Jack Hobbs, Herbert Sutcliffe, Hedley Verity, Douglas Jardine, Bill Bowes, Patsy Hendren, and the rest, I was bitterly disappointed. My day would be nearly ruined.

I never forgot this early experience and years later, when my turn came to captain England and to travel abroad as my schoolboy heroes had done, I was determined to give every consideration to the journalists accompanying the team. I tried never to lose sight of the fact that the task of the cricket Press is to supply a vast cricketing public in England with constant news of the game's leading exponents.

In my opinion, full Press conferences on cricket tours are outmoded, and almost useless. Every journalist much prefers a chat with the Test team captain—not with the vice-captain, manager or baggage-man. The one whose views matter most to the Press is the captain and a facility for personal contact with him is most important to them. Newspapermen do not want to be told collectively the same thing; each hopes for something different and as each has to satisfy a particular editor, I hold that the captain should try to give each man individual consideration.

Because of this, the leader of an England touring team needs to be—as well as a cricketer—something of a diplomat, speech-maker, and public relations officer. Above all, he is fortunate if he has a sense of humour. Without it he will be 'clean bowled' before the ship reaches port.

When I led the M.C.C. side to the West Indies the team was accompanied by Alex Bannister (*Daily Mail*), Charles Bray (*Daily Herald*), Peter Ditton (*Express* News and Features), Reg Hayter (Reuters & Press Association), Frank Rostron (*Daily Express*), E. W. Swanton (*Daily Telegraph*) and Crawford

White (*News Chronicle*). Each was required to do a different type of job and I did my best to co-operate with each and everyone of them. I did not concur with every opinion expressed by all of them but theirs was just as important and just as difficult a task as that of the players—perhaps more difficult. The following year the Press team which went with the M.C.C. team to Australia was far bigger. That party consisted of:—

John Arlott (*Evening News*)
L. N. Bailey (*The Star*)
Alex Bannister (*Daily Mail*)
John Bapty (*Yorkshire Evening Post*)
Denzil Batchelor (*Picture Post*)
E. A. Bedser (Free-lance)
Bill Bowes (*Yorkshire Evening News*)
Charles Bray (*Daily Herald*)
F. R. Brown (*Daily Mail*)
Neville Cardus (*Manchester Guardian*)
Harry Ditton (*News of the World*)
A. E. R. Gilligan (Broadcasting)
Alf Gover (*Sunday Pictorial*)
Ross Hall (*Daily Mirror*)
Bruce Harris (*Evening Standard*)
Margaret Hughes (*Sydney Daily Telegraph*)
John Kay (*Manchester Evening News*)
J. M. Kilburn (*Yorkshire Post*)
Ian Peebles (Kemsley)
Norman Preston (Reuters, Press Association)
Ron Roberts (Free-lance)
Alan Ross (*Observer*)
Frank Rostron (*Daily Express*)
Denys Rowbotham (*Manchester Guardian*)
E. W. Swanton (*Daily Telegraph*)
E. M. Wellings (*Evening News*)
Crawford White (*News Chronicle*)
Peter Wilson (*Daily Mirror*)
John Woodcock (*The Times*)

It is impracticable for me to mention all the cricket Press of the world by name, but I would like to express my particular appreciation of one who has been my closest contact and my best friend all through my life as a cricketer—John Bapty, of the *Yorkshire Evening Post*, a cricket correspondent for well over twenty-five years.

How delighted I was to see John walk into the Adelaide hotel the night England had retained the Ashes in Australia in 1954–55. He had witnessed a dream of mine come true. His round, jolly face beamed with pleasure—and when John beams there is hardly a finer sight.

In print, John has many times pointed ways in which I might have played better cricket. Surely that is his prerogative. But he has never used his friendship to tell me off the field what to do on the field. For this, I have always been grateful to him. May the newspaper offices of Britain continue to produce the like of John Bapty.

Every first-class cricketer should appreciate that newspaper reports of matches are not intended primarily for him. He should, I suggest, cut them out so that, when he has put away his bat and pads, he can read them again and reflect.

One that I still treasure is dated more than twenty years ago. In it, Frank Stainton of the *Leeds Mercury* wrote: "Hutton shows distinct possibilities of becoming an all-rounder." It was one of the first times I saw my name in print and the words gave me confidence, and inspired me to put a little more into my play.

Sometimes, of course, I have read things about myself which were scarcely likely to increase my confidence, though I appreciate that they may have been written in the best possible spirit.

Not long after I became captain of England, I read in a newspaper: "One Hutton in the England team is enough." Rightly or wrongly, I took this to mean that I was trying to mould other players on the same lines as myself. It upset me particularly because I felt very strongly at the time that the future of English cricket depended largely on our most promising young batsmen eradicating the weaknesses in their technique which I was sure the Australians would discover in five minutes.

These young men had not had the severe early training which I had received and which young Australians usually

I wish I liked cake. Hazare (India) and Hassett
(Australia), help in the cutting

I do like cups—Sportsman of the Year Trophy presented by Lord Burghley

Safe, if you keep it down

have before they reach State standard. It seemed to me an essential part of my duties as captain to try to help them from my own considerable experience.

If there had been even two more top-class batsmen in the country, England would have won more Tests than she did after the war and would almost certainly have won the 1950–51 series.

I have, I hope, made clear my respect and admiration for our English cricket correspondents. But, while on the subject of batting, I should like to submit one thought, which always comes to me when I read that a batsman has 'failed'. A bowler can bowl some bad overs and still meet with success. His mistake may cost four runs, it may go unpunished, even unnoticed. At any rate, he has another chance. But there are not many 'other chances' for a batsman in Test cricket. He is exposed very much to the whims of fortune and should, I feel, never be condemned too hastily.

J

CHAPTER XVI

'THE BOY FROM PUDSEY'

PUBLIC SCHOOLS are able to offer the best facilities and every encouragement and incentive to young cricketers. The staffs often include many masters who have won sporting distinction at either Oxford or Cambridge, and the youngsters are given the best coaching on some of the finest grounds in the world. Moreover, the boys have ample time for recreation.

Why, then, do the Public Schools not produce as many first-class cricketers as in the past?

Admittedly, the two most successful young English batsmen of the day, Peter May and Colin Cowdrey, come from Public Schools. But they are well ahead of their amateur contemporaries and must be considered exceptions to the rule.

It may be that fewer public schoolboys nowadays can afford the time for first-class cricket after they leave school. But in my view the main trouble is over-coaching. A certain amount of coaching is essential, but for any cricketer in England to be consistently successful over a period of years, he must possess a degree of inherent ability which the coach must be most careful not to stifle. I'm afraid too many of those who instruct the young tend to make the born games-player do something 'unnaturally' so as to conform with the orthodox theory.

There can be no substitute for genuine aptitude and tremendous enthusiasm. Take my case as an example. My parents were far from rich and they could not give me a Public School education. But I played cricket every moment when I could persuade anyone to join me—and my fervour for the game had, in those days, no such distractions as radio, TV, speedway and so on.

I was eleven when I joined Pudsey St. Lawrence, and in my first season with them I spent every evening, Monday to Friday, practising as hard as I could. I shared a special practice net with a number of other boys of my age and we made our own rule that no batsman should be 'out' until his stumps had been hit—which brought about some odd happenings. For instance, I began batting one Monday evening, continued on Tuesday and was still 'in possession' when we adjourned on Friday. I reckon I was at the wicket for about ten hours.

When I underwent the biggest endurance feat of my cricket career I batted for two and a half days at the Oval— 1938—reaching the record Test score of 364, against Australia, more than once my mind flashed back to that juvenile marathon. At least I had started to practise early the art of staying a long time at the wicket.

And, after all, if you think of it, possession of the crease is ten parts of the law of batting. I tried to convey this to one young player who asked me for some tips about going in first. I hope he understood that I was trying to help and not to be unkind or to over-simplify the matter when I replied that the main idea was just to 'keep mucking along'. Think it over there's a lot of truth in those words.

In my first game for Pudsey St. Lawrence second team against Saltaire at the age of twelve I went in number eight. No special equipment was provided for young 'uns like me, and I had to use a bat several sizes too big for me. Every time I tried a scoring stroke the handle jabbed into my middle, and after a few minutes I heard the opposing captain urge his fast bowler: "Go easy on him, he's only a bit of a kid."

The bowler responded to his captain's words and began to bowl to me less quickly than before, but I think that after a time he must have felt that my oversized bat was nearly as broad as long! He returned to his quicker pace, but, by that time, my eye was in and I was not easily shifted.

That was twenty-seven years ago, but I would like to thank that captain and bowler, whose names I have forgotten, for their consideration in giving me a chance to overcome my youthful anxiety. In later, more strenuous years, on cricket grounds far removed from Saltaire, I would have appreciated a few more of their types to provide me with such an encouraging start to an innings!

Nerves are the constant companion of almost every cricketer and are most difficult to shake off. Some batsmen talk a great deal in the dressing-room before going out. Others, including Sir Don Bradman and W. H. (Bill) Ponsford, those phlegmatic Australians whom I admired so much as a boy, managed to remain perfectly quiet. I am told that neither became the least flustered.

This is in keeping with a theory of mine that the player who can rise above nerves may *lose* colour from his face at critical moments, through pent-up determination to overcome his feelings, but *never* goes red. This may seem to you an extraordinary way of judging a cricketer, but I can assure you that in my experience it has worked pretty well.

If I see a cricketer, especially a batsman, with a flushed face just before he faces a moment of crisis, I have little confidence that he will overcome his nerves. Recently, England played a batsman who was always redder in the face when he walked out to bat than at normal times. Much as I hoped for his success, I was not surprised at his failure, or at the success he had when he returned to county cricket, which did not affect him so acutely.

I think the 'pale face' has sufficient grip on himself to master nerves, even when the pressure is full on.

The cricket I played as a boy was hard and always highly competitive. I am sure it did me good. I know of no easy path to the top in this exacting game. The only way is that which demands the utmost enthusiasm and the greatest concentration and I don't think I would have been as successful had I learned the game in other circumstances than the keenly competitive environment in which I was brought up. Only in tough conditions can a thorough knowledge of cricket be acquired, in all its aspects, and ability fully developed.

In one week of the school holidays I played in five matches —for none of which had I been selected! I achieved this by hanging around the door of the pavilion on the Pudsey ground hoping the local sides would be a player short, as almost invariably they were.

The moment a head popped out of the dressing-room door to look for a substitute, I was in like a flash!

I loved those matches, even though often I neither batted nor bowled. But cricket did not finish for me with the final drawing of stumps for the season. Many times in the winter I retired to a quiet corner of the house and practised strokes

with my well-oiled, well-used bat—my proudest possession—
and all winter I studied every cricket book I could find.

I believe also that the critical, yet friendly, attitude of the
Pudsey spectators, who seemed to expect a half-crown's worth
of entertainment for every sixpence charged for admission,
helped me a good deal. Their criticism, always well-intended
and based on a sound knowledge of the game, fitted me for
the sterner task of standing up to the varieties of criticism I
have met in county and Test cricket.

Two years after my Pudsey debut, I made the pilgrimage
to that Mecca of all potential Yorkshire county cricketers—
Headingley—for a trial in the indoor nets.

At fourteen, I felt very self-conscious as, carrying a cricket
bag, I walked through the snow-laden streets of Leeds on a
cold night in February.

When I reached Headingley, not a blade of grass was to
be seen. Everything was blanketed by snow. The only sound
disturbing the silence was of bat meeting ball in the nets, where
I met the illustrious George Hirst, then the county's chief
coach.

"You're the boy from Pudsey aren't you? Keep your eyes
open and you'll be all right," was George's greeting to me.
I changed into flannels and waited—with the kind of feeling
in my stomach that most people have when they sit in a
dentist's consulting-room.

I had gone to my first trial with plenty of trepidation, but
not without confidence. At my turn to bat, I quickly discovered
that one of George Hirst's most priceless assets as a coach was
that he always encouraged the player and never, never discouraged anyone. This imprinted itself on my mind, and I am
sure that everyone who has the responsibility of looking after
a young player should emulate George's example.

The coach who is always stopping a boy to point out faults
can discourage him so much that the pupil will reach the
stage where he becomes afraid to do *anything* in case he does it
wrongly; in his confused mind springs only a desire to escape
from his coach.

One county coach with whom I came into contact was a
retired schoolmaster and, because he gave his services, I would
be churlish to criticize him too severely. Yet every few balls,

he came down the pitch to tell me something, and I am sure he did nothing to build my confidence. Although I listened carefully enough, I cannot remember following his advice. This, perhaps, was the first instance of my later insistence on accepting advice on cricket only from those who had been 'under fire'.

Thank goodness, George Hirst was of different breed. He was easily the best coach I ever met, always punctuating his advice with remarks which increased, not decreased, my anxiety to play the game as well, and as often, as I could. He made me feel I was better than, in fact, I was—surely, the art of good coaching.

Like everyone else in charge of boys learning a game, George had some amusing experiences. Once, when he was coaching at Eton, a Second Eleven boy went to him and exclaimed, in all seriousness; "Excuse me, Mr. Hirst, but could you show me how to bowl a shooter?"

At first, George was tempted to tell the lad of the old gag the important thing was to spit on the ball; but his good nature prevailed; he told the truth, that a shooter was the result of some defect in the pitch, and not the outcome of any special human skill.

Many young bowlers who play on park pitches, however, still believe that shooters can be produced at will. They don't discover their mistake until they play on true wickets, where the budding young Larwoods begin to realize that bowling is not so simple, that something more than uncontrolled pace is required to beat the best batsmen.

Before leaving the subject of 'shooters' I would like to tell of the occasion when a fervent young Yorkshire supporter told George Macaulay he would reveal to him the hidden secret.

George made a show of being impressed, warned his confidant against any other bowler hearing about it and suggested they met on the county ground at seven o'clock next morning. Whether the conveyer of this vital information arrived at the appointed hour was never discovered. You see, George forgot to put on his alarm clock!

George Macaulay was one of the most colourful characters in Yorkshire cricket. Once, when fielding short leg to his bowling at Lord's, in a match against Middlesex, I stood no more than three yards from the bat.

Suddenly, George, whose accuracy was usually impeccable, bowled a full-toss which Patsy Hendren hit like a rocket past my left ear. Had it hit me, it could have done me serious damage. Instead, it crashed against the boundary fence. When it did so, I glanced round at George. With hands on hips he was glaring at me, and angrily he demanded: "Who's tha' peeping at?"

Perhaps not generally known is the story of George Macaulay and his lumbago pills. Once when George was laid low by lumbago, a former county captain gave him pills which eased the pain, and, physically speaking, straightened him out. George was so impressed he decided to make his own pills and put them on the market. He found a chemist friend who made up the pills for him and for a time business was good.

Then, suddenly, Mac's 'gold-mine' went out of production —he had been stricken with lumbago again, and was confined to bed!

George Hirst and George Macaulay were tremendous Yorkshire enthusiasts for the game. So, too, was Wilfrid Rhodes, who became coach at Harrow School after his retirement from first-class cricket. One day, he was bowling in the school nets to P. M. Studd, who repeatedly ran down the wicket to him. Then the batsman missed the ball, an error which would have got him stumped in a match. He looked highly amused, but Wilfrid did not share the joke. "You don't play this game for 'foon', Mr. Studd," declared Wilfrid with a frown.

Before I played my first game for Yorkshire, George Hirst warned me: "Don't forget, lad, it's entirely up to you now. I can't help you out in the middle."

How true that was! On the field, a player has only himself to rely upon. If he has been properly taught and encouraged, he has acquired the correct basic methods to add to natural ability, but, in match play, he alone can apply them.

Not that I was left on my own after George Hirst had passed me fit for county duty. I soon found players ready to advise and encourage me. One, Colonel Chichester-Constable, captain of the Yorkshire Second Eleven for whom I made my

debut when seventeen, had an innate flair for leadership.
Moreover, he understood the value of encouragement—
keeping to my theme that encouragement is almost more
important than any other factor.

Then there was Brian Sellers, under whose captaincy I
first played in the county side. Sellers, one of the most forthright people I have met, set an inspiring example.

When I began county cricket, I was lucky to play in the
same team as Hedley Verity and Bill Bowes. They, too, did
all they could to help me. And, in the evenings, the talk always
turned to cricket.

I feel that, except during very tense Test matches when a
change of subject may be a form of relaxation, too few players
today talk enough about the game off the field. Even now,
I never *stop* talking about it. And I am always ready to offer
advice to any player who comes to me.

Sometimes I have been most disappointed when a young
man who has just made his way into a county, or even a Test
side, has not sought guidance from experienced colleagues. I
am sure he would have found it given to him willingly. The
encyclopædia of cricket is not a closed book. The knowledge,
history and enjoyment of the game should be available to all,
and I know of no cricket 'Don' unready to pass on all he
knows. There are no trade secrets in cricket.

To all young cricketers I say: "Do not be discouraged by
early failure—and if things go wrong, don't blame your coach.
Look nearer home for the cause."

I take great interest in the welfare of all young cricketers
and do everything within my power to encourage them. This
applies above all, of course, to my sons, Richard and John.
Considering that once last season I took ninety minutes,
bowling leg-breaks and googlies on the lawn, to dismiss
thirteen-year-old Richard, elder of the two boys, he is hardly
likely to blame me in later years for lack of encouragement!

Unfortunately, with the ever-increasing tempo of modern
life—call it jet-age jitters, if you like—the demand for speed
appears to be uppermost in the minds of most young people.
They are constantly searching for something quicker and
better. Often, in the end, they find that what they get is
slower and inferior!

Batting on the matting in Bermuda

M.C.C. players on West Indies Tour 1953–54

A shot through
the Pakistan
leg trap at the
Oval, 1954

Cricket doesn't lend itself to this hurly-burly, and never will. The youngster of today who is enthusiastic about the game and enters it in the right spirit will obtain as much exercise as he needs on any one day and he will find it is as exciting as any other form of amusement. Cricket doesn't always sprint along but when the last ball is about to be bowled, it's four to win and the last man in, I think everyone on the ground is gripped by a feeling that doesn't come over the spectator of any other sport. And, as for the players, they are afire with tension. Take all the excitement of such happenings in a club match and multiply it by a hundredfold for a similar situation in a Test match—then you may capture some of the pent-up feelings on the field. Particularly if Jim Bloggs drops a sitter!

I imagine every adult spectator, who is a genuine follower of first-class cricket, will confirm that he has had his money's worth during the past five years. In my opinion, he will get more in the immediate future without any drastic revision of the present laws.

There is little wrong with cricket except the l.b.w. rule, to which I have referred already. But it is well known that some county clubs rely largely on income from Test matches to keep their teams in the field. From time to time, many suggestions have been made to relieve the financial worries of these counties. One which springs readily to mind is Sunday cricket, the idea apparently being to start county matches on Saturday and finish them the following Monday, ensuring two holiday 'gates' per week.

Organized Sunday cricket involving the leading players in England will never receive my support. Today, county cricketers in the top bracket find little opportunity for a few hours with their families. Sunday—then only occasionally— gives them that one chance and a day off during the week would hardly compensate them for the loss of their rest day on the Sabbath.

To attempt to rest when everybody else in this workaday-world is active is not at all my idea of rest and never will be, unless I manage to find a suitable spot somewhere in the middle of the Sahara! I became a restless type after years of cricket and thousands of miles of travel over many continents, and the noise of traffic alone was sufficient to create within me a craving for activity. So how could I have rested from my labours on, say, Friday?

When I was a boy I was made to go to Sunday school and church every week. Like most boys I was not particularly keen about doing so at the time but I have been very grateful since to my parents for putting me on the right path.

I think my approach to religion is roughly that of the average Englishman, respectful without being fanatical. But I do feel very strongly about Sunday cricket and I think that the British way of life, even its character, would be seriously threatened if the administrators of our great game allowed county and international cricket on the day of the week traditionally set aside for rest and worship. No Sunday cricket, *please.*

CHAPTER XVII

CRICKET AND GOLF

ALTHOUGH I have retired from first-class cricket, I hope to play a good deal of golf in the future and even to take part in minor competitions. On the subject of golf as a relaxation for the active cricketer, however, I'm afraid I am less enthusiastic.

When I was a boy I played golf near my home with a mashie and any old golf ball that I could find. In subsequent years I played a fair amount of golf and, before I broke my arm, I was playing to scratch.

Even so, I do not like to see youngsters who promise to be good batsmen devoting their time to golf. The swing of club and bat are so different that there is a strong tendency for one to ruin the other.

This is particularly the case when a boy acquires, at an early age, a good golf swing, with its groove. In batting there is no place for a groove, since every ball bowled requires a different approach.

The golf swing will also have brought with it a high back-swing; in batting the longer the back-lift the more chance there is of a mistake. There is little time to swing high if you are facing Lindwall and Miller in full spate.

The champion boxer does not draw his arm a long way back to gain the maximum amount of power. He develops a punch which travels as short a distance as possible.

So it should be with batting. If you can reach the boundary by taking the bat back shoulder-high, why go higher?

There have been times at the end of a day under the Australian sun when I have been very thankful that I have not acquired the habit of lifting the bat high. It can seem very heavy sometimes.

As I have said, the young batsman who has spent time becoming proficient at golf begins his cricket under a severe handicap. But I do not think the reverse applies. I see no reason why a good batsman should not take up golf at the age of, say, twenty-five, and, with a reasonable amount of practice, get down to a single-figure handicap.

I would submit that, whereas it must be possible for a gifted games player to perfect, with practice, the iron shot from the hanging lie, or the 'explosion' from a bunker, it is vastly harder to master the bouncers of Ray Lindwall or the googlies of Bill O'Reilly. You see, one can have next to no practice against them. Neither of these gentlemen was ever very enthusiastic about bowling to me in the nets, and quite rightly so. I had to learn about them in the middle as best I could.

No doubt it all comes down to the simple fact that in one game the ball is moving and in the other it is not.

*   *   *

While I was captain of England, I was always anxious that my players should not take golf too seriously. During that time I played little myself.

But I must admit to many hours spent on a variety of lovely golf courses during my travels as a first-class cricketer. Cricketers owe much to the officials of golf clubs both in England and in the Commonwealth. The hospitality I have received through the years has been wonderful.

The stories of incidents on golf courses come flooding back through my memory. There is one about the Surrey team who, during a Yorkshire v. Surrey match at Headingley, were invited on the Sunday to Sand Moor Golf Club. The Sand Moor and Moortown courses are adjacent and, after playing sixteen holes at Sand Moor, the party unwittingly played the eighteenth at Moortown and adjourned to the club-house.

This seemed curiously unfamiliar but nobody bothered very much until they tried to find their clothes. I believe it was Sandy Tait, the masseur, who finally decided that this was a different club-house and began the inquiries which led them back to Sand Moor.

Then my thoughts go back to South Africa in 1948–49, when the golf stories usually seemed to revolve round Jack Young. Once he drove a ball through the window of a member's car which was in the car park, well wide of the tee. He approached in some trepidation full of apologies, but the owner swept these aside, and insisted that Jack explain over a drink how he had achieved so wide a shot.

On another occasion in South Africa Jack's drive rebounded off the box on the ladies' tee some thirty yards away. As the ball ricocheted back Jack swung at it, caught it on the volley and cracked it 230 yards down the fairway, as far, and certainly as straight, as he had ever hit a drive before.

Happy days! In a way too happy, for there is always the temptation, particularly during the sterner Test series, that the cricketer will come to like his golf better than his cricket. And that will never do.

CHAPTER XVIII

SIX GREATEST BATSMEN OF MY TIME

I HAVE been asked so many times, both in private and public, to name the greatest batsmen and the greatest bowlers of my time that I feel I shall evade something expected of me if I fail to make my selection—repetitive as the idea has become.

I have been privileged to play with or against many great batsmen and I find the task of selecting the six best very difficult. However, if it has to be done, here they are:—

1. Walter Hammond (Gloucestershire and England)
2. Donald Bradman (Australia)
3. Denis Compton (Middlesex and England)
4. George Headley (West Indies)
5. Herbert Sutcliffe (Yorkshire and England)
6. Maurice Leyland (Yorkshire and England)

Walter Hammond

Walter Hammond was the finest player I ever saw on all types of wickets. I was never happier than when I was his partner, at the 'running end', as it were, and could watch him in action. This helped me to learn a great deal. Wally had that little extra something all the time, a gift bestowed on so few players. I cannot think of anyone of the same wonderful class.

Hammond had an extremely agile brain, which was the reason behind his amazing quickness into position for any type of stroke. Time and again he defied the first principles of the game by making up his mind where to hit the ball before it had left the bowler's hand, and he was good enough to get away with this cricket 'crime'.

Often he would make a shot that would cause the opposing captain to move a fielder to a particular spot to cut off the next stroke there. While the bowler walked back to his mark, Wally would look round to find a gap somewhere else. Having found it, he would send the ball clean through. That was Hammond at his majestic best.

I have never seen any other batsman so much in command of every situation as was Hammond when his eye was in. From the moment he walked from the pavilion to begin his innings, he looked the master. Such a giant of the game seemed always to dwarf the rest of the team, and the moment he faced up to bowling that had held difficulties for the other batsmen, that bowling appeared to lose its venom. Such was the illusion created by the magic of his peerless strokes. Hammond, in fact, made batting appear ridiculously easy, and it never is that.

Hammond was captain of England when I made my 364 against Australia. When I reached my first hundred, I thought the time had come for me to accelerate. Hammond straightaway sensed my intentions, came to the edge of the Oval pavilion balcony and signalled for me to keep my head down.

Maurice Leyland, my partner at the time, walked down the wicket to warn me that "the skipper wants you to go steady".

Eight years later, in Australia in 1946–47 when Hammond was again captain of England, he called me into his room before the start of the Second Test and asked if I would like to bat lower in the order. He had a suspicion that Ray Lindwall and Keith Miller would try to 'bounce' me out. We agreed, however, that where ever I went in to bat against Miller and Lindwall, I would 'get it in the neck', so it was as well I should take my 'medicine' in the number one position at which I was accustomed to bat.

Once, while we were batting together for England, Walter larruped a ball that hit me in the small of the back just as I turned to regain my crease. He chuckled at my frantic attempts to get out of the way, and I imagine I must have looked very comical from the other end of the wicket. Yet, when in the middle in charge of the fielding side, he was an unusually quiet, almost taciturn, man. I recall very few occasions when he spoke to anyone on the field, and only once when he said anything to me of any moment.

That happened in South Africa during the 1938–39 tour. Doug Wright, of Kent, was bowling against Dudley Nourse, and I thought that, if I moved some thirty yards, I would be in a better position to stop Dudley's favourite pull. I moved there and stayed in my self-appointed position for just two overs. Then Wally called me to him and, rather in the manner of a schoolmaster, told me not to move again unless he gave instructions. I never did!

The best innings I saw by Hammond was his 240 against Australia in the Second Test at Lord's in 1938. Charlie Barnett, Bill Edrich and I were out quickly—all to Australia's fast bowler, Ernie McCormick—for thirty-one, and Hammond started his innings when McCormick, then at top speed, must have felt he was on the point of running through the England side.

The confident way Wally played him soon put an end to any such idea and dispelled for me any suggestions that Wally was unhappy against bowling of extreme speed.

Another theory was that he was susceptible to 'bouncers'. I maintain that no batsman likes 'bouncers', and that, when bowlers resort to them, they are indirectly paying a compliment to the batsman. Thus, if Hammond received more than an average share of 'bouncers' in my view the bowlers were recognizing his greatness.

As captain of England for seventeen of the Tests in which I played, Hammond never asked any member of his team to do anything he could not do himself. He was an expert in every phase of the game.

Donald Bradman

Don Bradman, later to be knighted for his contribution to cricket, reached the heights of success on perfect batting wickets. As I cannot remember seeing him on a rain-affected wicket, I cannot place him as *the* greatest of all batsmen of my time, a distinction I have already accorded to Walter Hammond.

On a pitch to his liking, however, Don Bradman was supreme. His execution of every stroke, with the exception of the cover-drive, was well-nigh perfect. He was particularly fond of forcing the ball past mid-on's right hand and straight past the bowler between the wicket and mid-on.

Bradman had no equal in the pull, which he played in a way so few other batsmen have been able to accomplish. Don

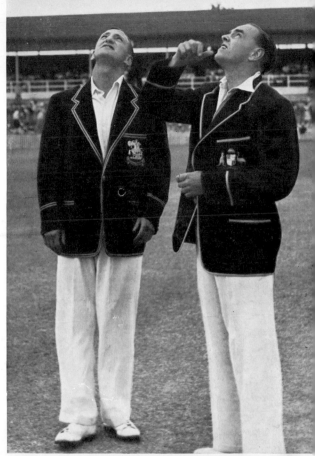

First Test toss with
Ian Johnson,
Brisbane, 1954–55

nly Godfrey Evans didn't
feel the cold at Perth

A cup of tea
from New Zealand'
Prime Minister

Deep-sea fishing
makes a break
from cricket

Husbands (Hutton
and Evans) and
wives return

always hit the ball *down*, bringing the bat with a downward swoop from high above the shoulder.

The majority of tip-top batsmen have small feet, enabling them to move extremely quickly, and Bradman was no exception. Indeed, he was the nimblest thing on two feet I have seen in cricket. Those tiny feet of his, governed by an unusually alert brain, were always in the right spot, with ample time to spare. If your feet are correctly in position you have taken the first step towards successful batting. Again, Bradman was able to lift his bat high for a forcing stroke, and yet move it only a few inches when defending.

Many cricket writers have referred to Bradman as an unorthodox batsman, but I claim that no batsman unorthodox in method can score over a hundred centuries in first-class cricket as he did.

If a good-length ball was pitched on his middle stump he would play it with his bat held as straight as any I have seen. When I was fourteen I saw him make 334 in an innings in the Leeds Test. Unorthodox? Not likely! Afterwards I went back to Pudsey and spent three hours practising, asking everybody I could find to bowl at me in the net. So there is a bit of Bradman in me, as well as Noble!

Ten days earlier, at Bradford, I had seen Don given out l.b.w. after scoring only a single against Yorkshire. Twenty-three years later, when he was in England as a correspondent with the 1953 Australian side, I asked him about this dismissal. In his typical Australian accent, he drawled: "I wasn't out, you know. I nicked it", meaning he had edged the ball on to his pad. He even remembered the name of the bowler, Emmott Robinson!

Don Bradman's intense concentration and gift for remembering the slightest detail were part of his extraordinary make-up. Once having faced a bowler, Bradman made a shrewd summing-up of his characteristics and, having done so, never forgot him.

He had that type of mind—cool logic was his great secret.

Denis Compton

If Don Bradman was described as unorthodox, what about Denis Compton? Denis often plays a straight ball with his bat

K

at an angle. His secret is an abundant natural aptitude and a gift for improvization that amounts almost to genius. Another great asset to him, I think, has been the fact that, though a right-handed batsman, he is a natural left-hander. He uses his left for bowling and throwing and the strength in it must have greatly helped his batting.

Denis and I each made a century on our first Test appearance against the Australians, at Nottingham, in 1938. I scored exactly 100, he made 102. Since then I have been associated with him in Test cricket more than any other player. Yet we have figured in so few long partnerships that I can count them on the fingers of one hand.

I can offer no satisfactory explanation for this, except that his best years, 1946–49, did not coincide with mine.

Through the years I have often watched with admiration Denis's skill on the rain-affected wickets which give the batsman his most searching test; and I have marvelled at his wide variety of strokes.

Denis plays every stroke in the textbook—many, too, which are *not* there—and makes the sweep shot consistently better than anyone I know. Many times I have seen him sweep the ball clean off his middle stump, and I just cannot remember a time when he has failed to connect. Even so, I confess that, when I have been batting with him, he has given me a queasy stomach every time he has made the stroke.

Still, results count in cricket, as in everything else, and bowlers who have tried to lure Denis into mistakes by over-use of his sweep stroke have not always enjoyed a later study of their analyses.

One of the most remarkable things about Denis is that, despite a series of knee troubles which would have finished most sportsmen, he has not only continued to play, but has never been left out of the England team, except once—at his own request.

As everyone knows, his misfortunes with that knee culminated in a winter operation for the removal of the knee-cap. At the moment of writing his cricket future is in the balance and, like everyone else, I sincerely hope he will be restored to fitness and able to resume his place in the England side which needs him so much.

George Headley

No boy could hope to bat like George Headley—'King George of Jamaica' and a law unto himself. Both his style and method of application were products of his youthful days in the sunny West Indies.

Headley was one of the few great players of my acquaintance who have not been good at driving off his front foot. Instead, he scored nearly all his runs by the square cuts, pulls and deflections, of which he was such a master. He had an open-chested, two-eyed—or rather, two-shouldered—stance, and anything short of a length he 'murdered'.

His wonderful eye for the ball allowed him to play it extremely late, almost at the moment when the bowler was about to appeal for leg-before. At that split-second, Headley's bat would descend on the ball like a flash.

Among Headley's many fine achievements was that of being the first cricketer to score two separate hundreds in a Test at Lord's, which he did with 106 and 107 in 1939. A noteworthy point about his scores was that, apart from him, only J. B. Stollmeyer (fifty-nine) made as many as thirty for the West Indies in either innings.

Headley, moreover, became the first player to score two hundreds against England twice. The other occasion he did so was at Georgetown, British Guiana, back in 1930.

In spite of apparent deficiencies in front of the wicket, Headley could play well in any conditions, a skill he must have developed through experience in Lancashire League cricket.

When a bowler begins to tire, he has a tendency to bowl shorter. Then, the magical bat of Headley would extract full toll. Yet, as cricket's most graceful shots are played to the well pitched-up ball, I always felt that, because of his disinclination to play off his front foot, Headley was never so attractive to watch as most of the other 'greats' of my time.

Herbert Sutcliffe

The best opening batsman with whom I was associated in my twenty-five years first-class cricket was Herbert Sutcliffe, a man who perfected the technique essential to every opening batsman—that of playing the swinging ball. Proficiency demands concentration of the highest order, and Herbert had more of this than anyone else I knew.

Furthermore, he possessed a magnificent temperament for the big occasion, unperturbed at anything that went on around him. Unperturbed, that is, except at one thing. He would not tolerate anyone moving in his line of vision as he was preparing to face the bowler.

When at the Nursery end of Lord's Sutcliffe would think nothing of waving his bat at M.C.C. members as a signal that their moving about in front of the pavilion distracted him. He considered that, as the man at the wicket, he had every right to request spectators in his line of vision to remain still. Only when satisfied that all was quiet and stationary would he get on with the game.

Most batsmen who play a bad stroke, or are beaten by a ball without being dismissed, are affected by the mistake. Not so Herbert Sutcliffe. He could be beaten five times in an over, but would play the sixth ball strictly on its merits, as if nothing untoward had happened.

Sutcliffe was not a gifted natural player like, for example, Denis Compton, but his temperament for the big occasion *made* him into a great player. He and Jack Hobbs were recognized as the finest England opening pair of all time and, although Herbert was not such an artist as his partner, his Test record bore comparison with that of anybody. His Test average of 60.73 was, in face, second only to that of Bradman (99.94).

Herbert hooked the ball splendidly but, because he made the stroke upwards (unlike Bradman) the Australians always set traps for him. In typical Herbert fashion, he never refused the challenge, because he reckoned that over a period he would score more runs by using his favourite stroke than by cutting it out of his repertoire.

Occasionally Sutcliffe lost his wicket hooking, but he took the risk with his eyes open, arguing that on the law of averages a batsman is most unlucky to be caught if he makes the hook stroke properly. As he rarely erred in his execution of the shot, the number of runs he scored with it more than compensated for the occasional lapse.

Maurice Leyland

I always enjoyed playing with that colourful Yorkshire character and left-handed batsman of renown, Maurice Leyland. In later years, after his retirement, I often wished Maurice was on my side, sitting in the pavilion waiting to go in to bat.

Maurice, of the chubby figure, ruddy countenance and placid disposition, exuded confidence, and was an ideal man in a crisis. In my first match for Yorkshire I was out for a duck and, naturally, was most disappointed as I made my way back to the dressing-room. The first person I met there however was Maurice, who exclaimed: "Don't worry, Lad, you've started at the bottom, I know, but you can't do worse—and you can do a darned sight better. We all know you will."

Although a master of presenting a dead bat to the ball, Maurice was extremely powerful, and when he brought his over-weight bat into action, the ball travelled at lightning speed.

His bats were so heavy that I would never try to use them. His liking for them was so well known by the rest of the Yorkshire team that once, when another member of the side saw, through a train window, a pile of railway sleepers, he remarked, aptly: "Look, a pile of Leyland cricket bats."

Maurice's stance at the wicket gave the bowler a better view of the stumps than most other players dared offer; yet he was a most difficult man to dismiss. Moreover, he was one of the few batsmen against whom that magnificent Australian, Bill O'Reilly, did not relish pitting his skill.

Once Maurice said to Walter Hammond: "I think I've got Bill O'Reilly taped, and I'm sure he knows it." And Maurice proceeded to follow words with action.

In the 1938 Test at the Oval, after Bill Edrich was out early, Maurice joined me. In Test matches he always wore his Yorkshire cap and, when O'Reilly, scanning the pavilion to see who his next opponent would be, spotted the White Rose cap coming through the crowd of spectators, he snorted: "It's that Yorkshire so-and-so again."

As Maurice and I put on 382 for the second wicket, O'Reilly's displeasure at seeing Maurice walk in to bat became amply justified. Once during the partnership, Maurice jokingly asked O'Reilly to bowl him a half-volley. Bill, always willing to take a gamble, retorted: "Yes, as long as you'll try to hit it for four!"

Bill dutifully obliged—and so did Maurice! Afterwards, Bill said to him: "You won't get another like that as long as you're in"—and he was again as good as his word. In the end, Maurice was run out for 187.

As he walked off the field, Neville Cardus stopped him and said: "Well played, Maurice, but I didn't think you were your usual carefree self." "Eh," replied Maurice, "but I'm playing for my place in this side." Maurice, indeed, had played in no other Test match in this series.

Just reflect on the batting strength of the England eleven at the Oval that year. After Bill Edrich and me, came Maurice Leyland, Wally Hammond, Eddie Paynter, Denis Compton, Joe Hardstaff (169 not out) and Arthur Wood (fifty-three) at number eight. England scored 903 for seven declared, but that didn't satisfy everybody. Certainly not 'Bosser' Martin, the Oval groundsman, who complained because England had not gone on for the 1,000!

*   *   *

Jack Hobbs has been omitted from my list only because he was finishing his career when mine started. Similarly, Patsy Hendren's cricket was coming to an end at the same time, and I did not see him in his prime.

CHAPTER XIX

SIX GREATEST BOWLERS

Now for the bowlers. I have selected as the best of my time:—

1. Ray Lindwall (Australia)
2. Bill O'Reilly (Australia)
3. Sonny Ramadhin (West Indies)
4. Hedley Verity (Yorkshire and England)
5. Alec Bedser (Surrey and England)
6. Keith Miller (Australia)

Ray Lindwall

The greatest bowler of my time undoubtedly has been Ray Lindwall. His intelligence, keen powers of observation and excellent physique have made him one of the hardest new ball bowlers to play, even though maybe today he is not quite the dynamic force he was between 1946 and 1951.

I first heard of Lindwall from Herbert Sutcliffe, who had been to Australia after the war on business. Herbert Sutcliffe told me that he had seen a young fast bowler in New South Wales with an action similar to Harold Larwood and who would, in his opinion, "give England's batsmen as much worry as Larwood gave the Australians before the war".

How right Herbert was in his prophecy was proved by subsequent events. When eventually I met Lindwall on the cricket field, he showed himself to be distinctly faster than any bowler I had met since long before the war. Because of his slightly low arm action, he released the ball from a position almost over the stumps. Very often the arm would be in direct line with the umpire, something I found to be most disconcerting, particularly if the umpire happened to rise from his stooping position at the same time as the ball was about to be released.

If Ray was to keep his arm higher at the moment of delivery,

167

many of the older cricket spectators could be forgiven for mistaking him for Harold Larwood.

Lindwall's two wicket-taking deliveries are (1) the out-swinger bowled at ninety per cent speed and (2) the yorker bowled at the leg stump with every ounce of energy he can put into it. The latter, used against the uninitiated, is the most dangerous ball I have yet played against. I have already related what happened to David Sheppard and his high back-lift.

Lindwall practised the bouncer tirelessly. This must be almost the hardest ball to bowl well in first-class cricket because, if it flies over the batsman's head, it is useless and should never take the wicket of a good player.

The bouncer which makes the batsman play a defensive shot is the most deadly one. Lindwall developed this short-pitched ball to perfection, inevitably following it up with his yorker or a ball well pitched up on or around the leg-stump.

His reputation was such that he obtained many wickets through cautious batsmen looking for his short-pitched ball and forgetting that he had something else up his sleeve. The short-pitched one was used when the occasion was favourable. It was a surprise weapon in the Lindwall armoury.

In Australia in 1946-47 the balls used in the Test matches had a form of varnish finish to them. After two or three overs the varnish would disappear. I well remember in the Second Test at Melbourne the varnished new ball reached me at the batting end, after Lindwall had released it, with a noise similar to a jet engine. He could certainly make the ball 'hum' at times.

In that same tour, a few weeks later in the Sydney Test, Lindwall bowled me the quickest ball I had experienced for seven years. The wicket was hard and fast, and an express delivery from him lifted off the pitch, flattened the index finger of my right hand against the bat handle and, for half a minute, paralysed the whole of my right arm. I glanced down the wicket and the glint in Lindwall's eye was a message I could not mistake—'I've a lot more where that came from!' How right he was!

Nowadays, Lindwall cannot sustain his pace as he did then, but he makes up in cunning for the loss of speed. Even if he gets slower still, there is no evidence that he will lose the ability to bowl English batsmen out!

Bill O'Reilly

In 1934 O'Reilly and Clarrie Grimmett swept through the England defences like a hurricane. That was my first year in county cricket and I did not meet Bill O'Reilly for another four years. In 1934, however, I well remember how, when the name of a prospective batsman for the England side came under the searching analysis of the Yorkshire county players, the first question always was: "Can he tell 'em?" i.e., can he detect the googly?

This conversation made a profound impression upon me and I promptly came to the conclusion that to play for England one must be able 'to tell 'em'.

At that time no one in the Yorkshire side, with the possible exception of Herbert Sutcliffe, could be sure of distinguishing the leg-break from the googly. Even Herbert was loath to say that he was certain. Yorkshire had no bowlers of the O'Reilly or Grimmett type, as they were not considered to be economic propositions in this county of hard-headed business men! It was, remember, the county of Peel, Rhodes, Hirst, Haigh, Verity and Macaulay, bowlers who imparted spin in accordance with the natural formation of the wrist and forearm.

From that moment, however, I made a detailed study of the art of playing leg-break and googly bowling. No textbook on cricket could have received more attention than I gave to the problem of tackling the great O'Reilly.

For four years I thought about it, often consulting those who had experience of batting against him. But not until Trent Bridge in 1938 did I discover his one big failing. Then, within fifteen minutes, I found out about his temper!

Every time his bowling was hit he would send down the next ball as quickly as possible. Accompanying the action would be a grunt and an exclamation that sounded uncommonly like "Take that you . . . !"

Despite his aggressive nature, I select Bill O'Reilly as one of the six greatest bowlers of my time. His physique was superb and he had the right sort of brain to go with it. His change of pace was most disconcerting. He was so unerring in his accuracy that it was difficult to make him alter the field he set so skilfully. Withal, he was a lovable character, who enjoyed his cricket intensely. Of all the Yorkshiremen against whom he bowled, I am sure, there are no two he 'cursed' more than Maurice Leyland—he did not like bowling to left-handers, to Maurice least of all—and myself.

Today Maurice and I are among Bill O'Reilly's best friends in this country and we look forward to his visits as a journalist covering the Australian tours here.

Sonny Ramadhin

The West Indies in 1950 brought to England a bowler almost unknown, even in his own country. Ramadhin was a chance selection who turned out to be a match-winner under English conditions.

His success then lay in his ability to conceal completely which way he was trying to spin. The difficulty of detecting his off-breaks from his leg had created doubt immediately in the mind of the batsman. Had we, the England players, not been so inquisitive in trying to detect the correct break the moment the ball left his hand we would have been more successful against him than we were. Small doubts increased to big doubts as match after match he tied up England's best batsmen.

As a youngster I was always taught to watch the bowler's hand. If watched closely and long enough, it should indicate to the batsman whether the ball is likely to be a leg-break, off-break or a googly. That is the general rule with most spin bowlers. But not so with Ramadhin. With a wrist as strong as steel, he delivers the ball quicker than any other bowler of his type.

Clearly it is a case of the hand deceiving the eye. I feel that there is some of the mystery of the East about his wrist action. In true Oriental fashion he is able to work a spell over many of his adversaries.

After his remarkable success against England in 1950, Ramadhin was given a good contract as professional with a Lancashire League club. The month of May, of the following year, was not a very encouraging one for him. The mystery man from Trinidad, who is of Indian descent, did not appear

to cause the once-a-week batsmen of Lancashire the problems
he had set for England's best. He was hit far and wide, hard
and often, by the blacksmiths, the bakers and the clerks of
Lancashire.

The following month, Yorkshire were playing at Bradford,
where a local league cricketer of my acquaintance stopped me
outside the dressing-room and remarked: "I see Ramadhin's
getting some stick int' Lancashire League." The tone of his
voice and the expression on his face could mean only one thing
—'What were you doing last year?'

But when the sun shone later in Lancashire, my inter-
rogator was given cause to change his tone, for then Ramadhin
was able to start his tricks. He finished the season with over
100 wickets, heading the averages, and breaking several league
records.

There is no doubt that Ramadhin is a fifty per cent better
bowler in England than elsewhere. Our wickets suit his type
of bowling admirably. The uncertain light at times, plus the
poor backcloth on so many grounds, has aided his guiles. In
England he becomes the illusionist working his deceptions
against a black background.

Hedley Verity

A wet month of May in the north of England could hardly
be other than a dismal opening to our county cricket season,
especially for any young player taking his first steps on the
long road to success. Yet those same conditions in the year 1931
enabled one to start his career in a blaze of glory, even if the
sunshine was missing.

He had bowled with great promise in a few matches the
season before. Now he swiftly justified the high hopes held of
him. In only the second championship match of the season he
took all ten Worcestershire wickets for 36.

It was the sort of beginning every young cricketer fervently
hopes for and so few ever get. The mantle of the great Wilfrid
Rhodes when he retired from first-class cricket had fallen on
the slender shoulders of Hedley Verity, his natural successor
in the Yorkshire side. Hedley wore it with immediate distinction, establishing himself so quickly as a left-arm slow bowler
of outstanding natural ability that the change-over, so far as

Yorkshire was concerned, was accomplished in a manner without parallel in my time.

Verity's great asset was height. Being six feet tall himself, he was able to command altitude at will. But he did not spin the ball as much as Charlie Parker of Gloucestershire, or Surrey's Tony Lock of the present day. Some observers even would add the name of Wilfred Rhodes.

It would be more accurate to say that Verity rolled the ball rather than spun it and, after four strenuous years of cricket at home and abroad, he appeared to lose a little of his skill. This was due, no doubt, to the heavy calls made upon him as a bowler on perfect batting wickets, on which there was little or no deviation of the ball after it had pitched.

This sort of thing can deprive any slow bowler eventually of the incentive to give the ball that little extra 'zip'. It applies particularly to those Englishmen who get results in this country by the use of spin applied only by the fingers and wrist. The great Australian spinners of the past used fingers, wrist and arm, plus that little extra something which the others hadn't got.

On one occasion, in my first year with the Yorkshire county side, I found myself in the slips to Verity's bowling alongside Arthur (Ticker) Mitchell. I think I must have missed a chance of catching someone, for it was only then that Mitchell noticed my presence. In his droll Yorkshire manner he muttered: "What's tha doing 'ere? It took me fifteen years to get int' slips."

In that match the pitch was responsive to spin but, for reasons quite unknown to the rest of us, Verity was not getting wickets. Those of you who know Yorkshire county cricket intimately will not have to be reminded of the consternation that reigns in the Yorkshire camp when the left-arm 'twiddler' fails, especially where the wicket is 'made to order'.

As one over succeeds another and the batsmen still stay there, nothing is said by the Yorkshire players; an exchange of glances is quite enough. This state of affairs has been known to extend itself beyond the playing field to the score box, the committee room and the Press benches in Yorkshire. It is inevitably the cue for reminiscences of what Rhodes would have done in the circumstances.

Verity's lack of success that day produced another typical remark from Arthur Mitchell. "Dusty," he said (meaning Wilfrid Rhodes, of course), "would have bowled 'em out on this wicket as fast as they came in."

It is not my intention to make comparisons between the two. Should anyone have any doubts about Verity's greatness as a bowler the record books will remove them. Let it suffice to say that we shall never see greater exponents of the art of slow left-arm bowling than Rhodes and Verity, although it is always to be hoped that some youngster of the present day has already been gifted with their qualities and will ultimately make his mark. At the moment, Johnny Wardle is proving himself a worthy successor so far as Yorkshire are concerned.

As a man, Hedley Verity was second-to-none on and off the field and a grand ambassador for cricket. He had a deep love for England and in the end, having served it so well as a cricketer and soldier, he laid down his life for his country in Sicily in 1943 while fighting as an infantry officer.

As an England cricketer, Hedley Verity made his last sea voyage aboard the *Athlone Castle* on the way back from the 1938–39 tour of South Africa. I shared a cabin with him on the journey and I remember that his constant companion was a little book entitled *Infantry Training*. I am certain he had a good idea then of what the immediate future had in store for all of us and where his own destiny lay. Yet he never spoke about it; cricket was his main topic of conversation. He hero-worshipped Wally Hammond and was never tired of talking about Wally's great talents as a player.

Hedley was serious-minded, almost taciturn at times, yet he could always stand leg-pulls at his own expense. In a match at Sheffield in 1935 H. B. Cameron, the South African batsman-wicket-keeper, hit Verity's bowling for three sixes and three fours in one over. At the end of it, Arthur Wood, the Yorkshire wicket-keeper, remarked consolingly: "At least you had him in two minds that over, Hedley." Verity smiled somewhat ruefully; he was not in the least bit upset.

Although I was not on the tour, I know that in Australia on another occasion when rain had fallen on the wicket Verity pressed his thumb into the turf in order to test it before bowling and with some satisfaction remarked: "Poor Don."

When, however, Don Bradman arrived out in the middle he proved singularly little in need of sympathy. Entirely unperturbed by the state of the wicket, he collected seventy runs in good time, to the amazement of Verity who had counted upon the combination of tricky wicket and left-arm cunning to remove the Don without much difficulty. Hedley often told this story against himself.

The incident I remember best, however, concerns myself. One day during the trip home from South Africa before the war Hedley took me on one side and said: "Now, you young devil, you haven't done too well on this tour. What are you going to do about it?" There was a twinkle in his eye as he said it and I, wistfully, promised to do better next time. It so happened that the approaching summer, that of 1939, was my best season in English cricket.

Hedley died from wounds received on the field of battle. I like to think that, had he lived, he would have been pleased that I, a fellow Yorkshire professional, came to lead England on those cricket fields he loved so well.

Alec Bedser

From 1948 to 1953 Alec Bedser was the finest mediumpaced bowler in the world on all wickets. Few cricketers besides myself in England teams since the war have seen more of this big-hearted man, who became an outstanding bowler of his time. That he succeeded, largely by his own efforts, is now common knowledge.

During the Test trial match at Lord's in 1946, Wally Hammond remarked to me: "I think this chap Bedser is going to be a very good bowler." That happened after Alec dismissed both of us. As events proved, Hammond's was an understatement.

In his first Test match, some ten days later, Alec took seven Indian wickets for 49 in the first innings and four for 96 in the second. I believe his first innings performance was, in figures, the best by any cricketer playing in his first Test.

He played in all three Tests that season, taking twenty-four wickets for just over twelve runs each, and he was an automatic choice for the side to go to Australia in the winter.

His experiences on that tour helped to make Alec the great

bowler he became two years later. In the course of it he
literally bowled himself to a standstill. What is more, he sent
down one of the finest balls I have seen bowled anywhere in
twenty-one years of first-class cricket.

The Adelaide Test match in February 1947 was played
during a period of intense heat. It was so hot at the time that
South Australia was 'burnt up'. It was too hot even for a cold
shower after cricket, if you understand my meaning.

Nevertheless, Alec bowled long and unsparingly. He put so
much effort into his bowling that, after one particularly
exacting over, he staggered from the wicket to an incorrect
position in the field, rather like a boxer going to the wrong
corner at the end of a punishing round. He was too exhausted
to notice his mistake, yet he carried on and was able,
miraculously, to produce the wonder ball that captured
Don Bradman's wicket. I have rarely seen the Don so
surprised.

I was fielding at mid-off and thus had an excellent view
of what happened. The ball was directed at leg-and-middle
but, late in flight, moved slightly to leg. Not too late, however,
to escape the eagle eye of Bradman, who shaped to run it to
the on side. It pitched round about the leg stump, broke sharply
and hit the wicket between the middle and off stumps.

Who was the more surprised, Don or Alec, I was not
certain; but I am sure that neither batsman nor bowler has
forgotten it. When Bradman was nearly back in the pavilion
Alec's face was still showing blank amazement. I had to remind
him that it had really happened—he had taken the Don's
wicket. Such was Don's confidence that I feel that *he* did not
believe it had really happened until he was sitting in the
dressing-room removing his pads.

As captain of England, I found Alec Bedser a grand type
of bowler to have under my command. He never appeared to
disagree with any suggestion I made to him on the field and he
rarely passed comment beyond an occasional: "The slips are
too deep," or "Take so-and-so out of the slips, he can't catch
'em."

As with Maurice Tate, so with Alec Bedser. He liked to
have the wicket-keeper as near to the stumps as possible. He
wanted something to bowl at; the batsman and the stumps

were just not enough for him. In this connection, of course, he was magnificently served by Godfrey Evans.

So often has Alec made the new ball swing away down the leg-side—always a difficult ball for any wicket-keeper—that Godfrey Evans has had to take many body blows coping with it. A black and blue forearm at the close of play was always a good indication of the number of byes Godfrey had prevented.

I know Alec would be the first to admit that, with Godfrey Evans keeping to him in Tests and Arthur McIntyre in county matches, he has had wonderful support.

Keith Miller

Keith Miller is the most unpredictable cricketer I have played against. I am never quite sure what he is going to do next and I don't think he knows himself until he is about to do it.

I first met Miller during the Australian Services team's tour of England in 1945 when the series known as 'Victory Tests' was played. In ten years since he has earned a ranking among the best all-rounders the cricket world had known.

As a bowler he did in 1945, and still does, something which I, as a batsman, never like to see—he holds the seam of the ball upright. On a bright day I have actually seen the seam vertical as the ball sped towards me. With this type of delivery I have always had to guess which way it would go after pitching. Sometimes it has moved inwards, at other times outwards; there has never been a sure way of telling.

I have never known a bowler who cared less about his bowling mark than Miller. He has bowled at me from a run-up of three yards. At other times, I have seen him run across towards cover to field one of his own deliveries, then carry on by running round mid-off into the straight and up to the bowling crease like a tornado.

Keith can bowl good off-spinners, leg-breaks, square-arm slingers and even the googly. He is, I repeat, unpredictable. Occasionally, he has bowled at me as if I was not worthy of his attention. Then, suddenly, there has been a transformation in him and I have needed every bit of concentration of which I was capable to counter the challenge.

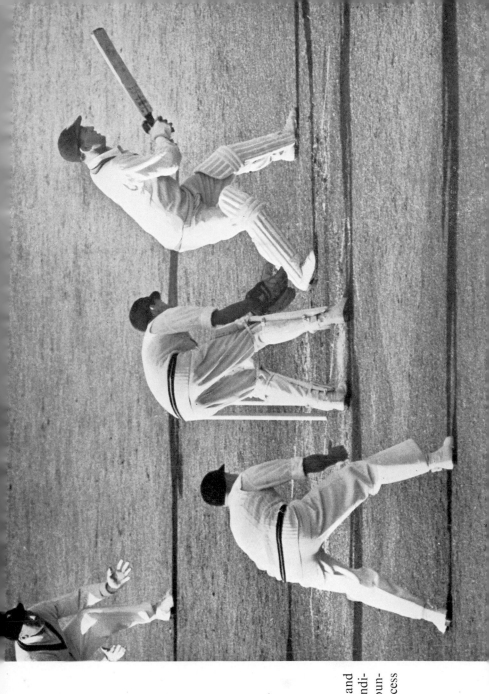

Chin, wrist, and foot in perpendicular line—a foundation of success

More tips for batting

He once said to me: "Len, if I could bat like you, I would give a bowler like me some stick." I replied: "Yes, and if I could bowl like you I'd give you some."

Keith thrives on the important occasion, yet I have known him in lesser games to be completely disinterested in the proceedings. One of the best examples was at Southend in 1948, when Don Bradman's team hit the Essex bowling for 721 runs in a six-hour day.

The Australians were 364 for two when Keith's turn came to bat—and that was only an hour after lunch. He was taking a siesta at the time and, on being aroused, protested that he was not keen to bat. When he realized that he had to go in, he marched out to the middle, scorned taking guard and, with bat still raised over his shoulder, was bowled first ball by Trevor Bailey whose analysis to that point was something like one for 100.

Take another, completely opposite, example of the unpredictable Miller. Ten minutes before tea on the first day of the Sydney Test in the 1950–51 series, England were 128 for one wicket and apparently coasting towards a big score.

Then Lindsay Hassett called upon Miller for a spell of bowling. He had been fielding on the boundary, spending part of the time chatting to a spectator, but the moment he started bowling he was as fast as I have ever known him to be. He got rid of first, me, then Denis Compton, in three balls and quickly followed by taking Reg Simpson's wicket. So from 128 for one, England suddenly were 137 for four. And all through Miller. Having virtually decided the match in a few overs, he went calmly back to his conversation on the boundary.

I think Miller's mood as a bowler depends to a large extent on how much he likes or dislikes the man at the other end, the one holding the bat.

During the many uncomfortable hours I have spent at the receiving end against his bowling, he has hit me three times, viz., twice on the shoulder and once in the stomach. I remember these incidents so well because there was no alternative but to take the raps—the pace of each ball was such that I had no time to get my bat anywhere near it.

Of all the bowlers who have hit me at some time or other during the past twenty-one years, Keith is the only one who

L

has made me feel that, whatever defence I had, it was useless at those moments.

He has the perfect action for a fast bowler, delivering the ball with his right hand high above his left hip, thereby obtaining the maximum amount of effort at the last possible moment. This enabled him, so it appeared to me, to gain more pace off the wicket than most other fast bowlers are capable of doing.

A grand sportsman in every way, he constituted with Ray Lindwall the most hostile combination of fast bowlers it has been my misfortune to face. To these two more than any other single factor do I attribute the cricket supremacy which Australia enjoyed for so long after the war.

CHAPTER XX

WORLD ELEVEN

THE logical successor in most people's minds to the Six Greatest Batsmen and Six Greatest Bowlers always seems to be a World Eleven. So here, from the players I have played with or against, is my modest attempt to solve another immensely difficult problem:—

1. Herbert Sutcliffe (England)
2. Cyril Washbrook (England)
3. Don Bradman (Australia)
4. Wally Hammond (England)
5. George Headley (West Indies)
6. Maurice Leyland (England)
7. Leslie Ames (England)
8. Keith Miller (Australia)
9. Ray Lindwall (Australia)
10. Hedley Verity (England)
11. Bill O'Reilly (Australia)

My eleven to oppose them would consist of the following:—

1. Sidney Barnes (Australia)
2. Arthur Morris (Australia)
3. Martin Donnelly (New Zealand)
4. Everton Weekes (West Indies)
5. Denis Compton (England)
6. Clyde Walcott (West Indies)
7. Godfrey Evans (England)
8. Jim Laker (England)
9. Bill Johnston (Australia)
10. Kenneth Farnes (England)
11. Alec Bedser (England)

Picking teams of this description can never be other than a matter of opinion, so that where the claims for inclusion in the World Eleven are particularly close, I feel I should explain my reasoning.

Herbert Sutcliffe would be my automatic choice for number one because he was a great player on all wickets and had the best technique against the new ball of any opening batsman I met. I have always regretted that I did not see his great innings on a 'sticky dog' at Melbourne in 1928, when he was partnered by Jack Hobbs. Their batting that day must have been something to remember all through life.

As Herbert's partner in my World Eleven, Cyril Washbrook may be a surprise choice to many. I have preferred him to Sidney Barnes as my number two because he was obliged, during his career as a Test player, to bat against a better attack than Sidney Barnes had to face at the same period. The Australian attack in 1946/48/50 was the best I have batted against. For instance, I have often thought how interesting it would have been to see how Don Bradman shaped against Lindwall, Miller, Johnston, Johnson and the rest.

Cyril Washbrook realized his own limitations in stroke play and confined his strokes to those at which he was best, but, like Herbert Sutcliffe, he was a splendid player on all types of wickets and, in addition, a fine fielder.

Sidney Barnes went out of first-class cricket much too early. Nevertheless he was a fine player, not even overshadowed by Bradman though, of course, the post-war Don was not quite the fantastic machine of the '30s. Barnes was a man I would always want to have on my side, for his sheer cricketing ability alone. Was there ever a shorter short-leg than Barnes? Whenever he fielded against me in that position, I was perpetually bothered by having him in the corner of my eye as the bowler was running up.

I found that the most difficult choice of all to make was between George Headley and Denis Compton. In the end, I plumped for Headley although I am positive it would not make a scrap of difference which of them went into my World Eleven. Finally Headley's fielding influenced me slightly in his favour. Compton, when completely fit, was a good fielder, but never brilliant as Headley was at cover point or in the gully. On the score of batting ability, however, it can be argued that through the years Headley had better wickets to bat on than Denis.

I have picked Leslie Ames instead of Godfrey Evans as wicket-keeper for the 'first eleven' because of his superior batting. Leslie scored 102 centuries, a wonderful achievement for a wicket-keeper. In the middle '30s he was one of the best batsmen in England, although he never did so well for England with the bat as his undoubted ability suggested he could. As a wicket-keeper, Leslie Ames was safe without being brilliant in the Godfrey Evans manner. But probably there has never been a better wicket-keeper-batsman.

H. B. Cameron, the South African, was extremely good but not in the same class as Leslie Ames and for that reason he misses selection for the 'second eleven' by the narrowest of margins. Godfrey Evans supplants him because he has taken catches behind the stumps which, in my opinion, no one else could have held. He has also played a number of useful innings in Test cricket.

With such a battery of bowlers as Lindwall and Miller as openers, Verity (slow left-arm), O'Reilly (leg breaks), and Wally Hammond, who was good enough to open the bowling for England at any time, I am obliged to relegate Alec Bedser to the 'second eleven'. Verity gets the vote over Bill Johnston because he was a much better batsman.

Two outstanding left-arm slow bowlers in the world at the moment are Johnny Wardle, of Yorkshire, and Tony Lock, of Surrey, neither is included in my World Elevens for two reasons; (1) they are not, at this stage of their development, better than Verity and Bill Johnston were at their peak; (2) they are certain to improve still further as they get 'older in the head'.

I have watched both Wardle and Lock make their start in first-class cricket, move steadily into the top class, and, finally, reach international standard. They have worked hard, in fact, nobody worked harder, to master the art of slow left-arm bowling, and they worthily uphold the great traditions handed on by such as Peat, Peel, Briggs, Rhodes, Parker, Blyth and Verity.

Of the two, Wardle has had the more difficult passage in having to follow in the Yorkshire side Hedley Verity and Arthur Booth. Booth headed the first-class bowling averages in 1946, but he is probably better remembered as the bowler who was told by his skipper to put his sweater on after bowling a no-ball! Yorkshire youngsters who bowl slow left-arm are not permitted the luxury of no-balls. Authority frowns upon such things.

Tony Lock, on the other hand, did not have to take over from an exactly similar type of bowler in the Surrey side and therefore could not be subjected to any such comparisons.

Johnny Wardle has been constantly plagued by being compared with Rhodes, Verity, etc., in Yorkshire, but it has done him more good than harm. From it has resulted a defiant 'I'll show 'em whether I'm as good as so-and-so was' attitude.

Wardle is made of sterner stuff than to be upset by comparisons with his Yorkshire predecessors and, no doubt, he often reflects that fifteen years hence his own name will be added to the list of those quoted at aspiring Yorkshire left-arm spinners.

Apart from his value as a bowler, Wardle has played some very useful innings in Test cricket. He made an invaluable contribution to England's victory in the thrilling Second Test at Sydney in 1954. On that occasion he devised his own batting technique, a highly revolutionary affair. Four or five balls per over he missed completely by anything between two inches and two feet. With others he connected and made runs off them. The shot which really foxed the Australians was the one where he both retreated towards the umpire and advanced towards the bowler, bat held aloft. He kidded them into believing that a straight drive was his intention. In fact, the ball nearly always flew over the heads of the slips! All this went very well with the crowd.

Some people will wonder why I have left out of my World Elevens the name of Athol Rowan, the South African, and given preference to Jim Laker. My answer is—because I feel that Laker spins the ball more than did Rowan. I have batted against both of them on a turning wicket and always found Laker harder to play.

Jim Laker would have been even more successful than he has already been had he not had the misfortune to be pitted against the tremendously strong Australian batting side of 1948. He had a particularly unfortunate match in the Leeds Test, in which Miller 'got after him' and smote him good and hard. It took Laker a long time to recover from that hammering.

Miller had also proved his undoing at Lord's, making seventy-four runs in quick time.

Those experiences in 1948 were not helpful to Laker early in his career as a Test cricketer. They gave a boost to Australian morale as far as his bowling was concerned, though he got some of his own back at the Oval in 1953.

As a candidate for the M.C.C. party to Australia in 1954–55 he clashed with Bob Appleyard and was extremely near to selection. Appleyard is what I would call a more direct type of bowler than Laker, in that he does not flight the ball so much. I have seen a lot of batsmen try to hit Appleyard off his length and fail. This immunity from punishment was largely responsible for the Selectors preferring him to Laker.

In Australia I tried to make sure that no one did master him, remembering what had happened to Jim Laker in 1948. Once or twice Keith Miller came in with the intention of 'belting' Bob but I was very careful not to let a situation of this sort develop.

For all the pros and cons surrounding the rival claims of Laker and Appleyard, I still consider that Laker is the best off-spinner on all classes of wickets during my time.

We have yet to see the best of Brian Statham as a fast bowler, which is why I passed him over and gave preference to Kenneth Farnes for the World Eleven. Whenever I think about Farnes, tragically killed while serving with the R.A.F. in World War II, I recall the Gentlemen and Players match at Lord's in 1938, in which he produced some of the most frightening fast bowling I have ever seen.

Farnes stood six feet five inches and brought the ball down from a height of something over nine feet. In that match he had been slightly put out over something or other and he gave vent to his feelings with his bowling. When Farnes was in that mood, it was better to be on the fielding side than to be facing him as a batsman. He was a very fine bowler.

Brian Statham's fine bowling on the last Australian tour was possibly the most consistently accurate since the days of Harold Larwood. Statham is a magnificent fielder into the bargain. The closeness of choice between Farnes and Statham is like that between George Headley and Denis Compton.

Which of my two World Elevens would I care to play against? The answer is—neither.

CHAPTER XXI

THE DAY OF RECKONING

To everyone at some time or another, comes a day of reckoning when we reach, as it were, the point of no return.

For me, that day dawned on Tuesday, 17 January, 1956, twenty-two years after my first appearance for Yorkshire.

I knew when I got up that morning that it was to be the day of decision and, as I got ready to see the specialist, I think I already knew the answer—though I still hoped for the best.

Surely, I had thought, as I turned the problem over in my mind during the anxious three weeks after I got out of my plaster-cast, I can go on, if only for two or three summers. The only thing above all I wanted was to have one final crack at the old friend and 'enemy'—the Australians.

Determined to give myself the most stringent test in the hope that my fitness would be proved, I had tried myself out in my garden with my two sons, John and Richard. We played lots of football, and they watched, solemn-eyed, while I skipped, skipped and skipped.

The exercise had given me the answer that even I, in my anxiety to carry on, could not deny. The pain in my back had returned, and, though it was only slight, I knew it meant I should be unable to stand up to the strain of cricket six days a week.

The specialist on that sunny January morning, after a long and thorough discussion, confirmed this. The risk of recurrence of my back trouble was too great.

*   *   *

After that, I had to face the truth—and to announce my retirement.

I had felt there *ought* to be a good deal more cricket left in me. But I felt, too, a sense of duty to the cricket public in general and to the Yorkshire club in particular. As I saw it, if I took the risk of going on, I should be receiving a year's pay for perhaps only a few weeks' cricket. And to me, that would have been taking money under false pretences.

I wanted, moreover, to go out on the top note. The perfectionist part of my make-up would not allow me to go on trying the impossible—tackling first-class cricket with second-class health. Frankly, I'd rather not play at all than merely potter along, a mere shadow of the Len Hutton the public would rightly expect to see.

It was only fair, too, that, in the circumstances, I should renounce any future claims to the England captaincy in favour of a younger, fitter man. There was always the possibility of my playing for Yorkshire and perhaps hitting a century or two—with a resultant clamour by some of the public for my return to the Test arena. And that would have created an impossible situation for everyone concerned.

When I had made the decision, I knew a peace and quietness of mind that had not been my companion for several years. I felt sure I had taken the right step, and with that certainly a relief that the struggle was over; an end to the strained muscles and taut nerves that had been more bitter enemies to me than any Australian!

But it was a bitter pill to swallow and that afternoon I somehow found myself thinking of those poignant words of Shakespeare: 'Parting is such sweet sorrow'.

It was good-bye to the hurly-burly, the thrills, the glamour, the excitement of the Test arena. Good-bye to that moment of pride as I faced up to the 'enemy' thundering up to the wicket bent on my destruction. Good-bye to the tense, eerie silence of the great crowd watching the battle; to the good-natured comment of the barracker echoing across the sunlit ground; to the happy trot back to the pavilion after a century well-earned, the unpadding in the dressing-room and the luxurious relaxation that goes with the feeling of a job well done.

Instead a seat at the ring-side and the task of trying to make myself content merely to play the role of an onlooker.

And that also means no more aspirins to lull me to sleep when pain after a long day in the field racks my body. It means escape from the sleepless nights that were inevitable companions after a specially arduous knock.

"Cricket is my life." So often have I said that and written it that the break could be nothing else than a terrific wrench.

The sweetness in the sorrow? Mainly in the feeling that if I can no longer give my all to cricket actively on the field, there is much that I can still give to the game in other ways.

Remembering my own struggles as a youngster, my problems and difficulties made the harder because of an innate shyness and reserve, I want, more than anything, to help young cricketers, particularly those fired with ambition similar to my own when I was just the 'boy from Pudsey'.

I think I can do a lot in that direction, to help, guide and encourage the young men destined to wear the England blazer in the years to come.

If I can succeed in that ambition, then retirement at a comparatively early age will have been worth while. To put something appreciable back into the game will be a return for what cricket has given to me.

Yes, the game has done much for me—and what greater honours could a cricketer retire with than the captaincy of England, and election as a life member of the M.C.C. while still playing as a professional?

The many friends—true friends—that the game has given me is another aspect of retirement's 'sweet sorrow'. Friends, not only in my beloved, native Yorkshire, or in the breadth of England outside the North, but in other countries. Even though I may not now see them much I feel they are still my friends.

But for cricket, I should never have seen the world as it has been my good fortune to do. True, the strain of modern cricket tours with their hectic, exhausting tempo, and their fierce glare of publicity, has probably contributed to my rather premature retirement.

But I have no real regrets, and if I could go back, I wouldn't change one thing. Always in my memory will live, vividly, the other side of those overseas tours—the fun and thrill and experience of three M.C.C. tours in Australia and New Zealand with Test teams and two M.C.C. tours each to

South Africa and the West Indies, besides my Yorkshire tour of the West Indies when I was eighteen. If I had had time to keep a diary—which I didn't—I could have written a book on each of those tours!

Given the chance again, I would skipper England, even if I had a broken leg and needed a runner when batting, and a substitute in the field! The worry of the task of captaining England is, to me, outweighed by its irresistible fascination. The sleepless nights and the uneasy stomach which heavy responsibility can cause are balanced by the satisfaction and 'kick' that come from Test leadership.

When there are no more sleepless nights, when the butterflies in the stomach stop fluttering, life begins to feel a little empty!

There is another side to my retirement—the effect upon my wife and my two sons. Now, at last, we can settle down to live together like a normal family. I know that Dorothy will miss the old life, because she has been my unfailing companion and inspiration, always understanding me to the full.

For her, it has been tough going, caring for my health, a home and a family, often playing the role of private secretary, with me at home one day and off the next.

While retirement for me means no more winters abroad except at my own choice, and no more summers away from Yorkshire, for Dorothy and the boys it means family weekends, a run to the coast, picnics and all the other homely things.

Perhaps my sons have been most affected by my cricket career, as witness John's remark to his mother when she told him the news of my retirement: "Good. Daddy will be home more now, won't he?"

As for my elder son, Richard, I think my decision brings with it disappointment that I shall not be taking part in any more Tests. Incidentally, one of his proudest possessions is an old Yorkshire sweater of mine which he managed to get into after Dorothy had washed it at home—and shrunk it!

The effect of my cricket on Richard during the past few years can be gauged from the fact that at Leeds, during the last Australian Test series, he saw me bowled for a 'duck', second ball, and promptly burst into tears!

My plans for the future? At the time of writing I have made no definite decision, but I hope to turn out for Yorkshire—as an amateur—in an occasional 'friendly' match.

Whatever I do I shall always carry with me the memory of England's triumph during these last few years. The satisfaction of having, in the evening of my cricketing career, helped her not only to regain but also to retain the Ashes will be something that time cannot take away from me.

THE END

INDEX